Special

The Commentary

Definitions, Clarifications, and Purposes

Patricia L. Johnson Howey, B.A., I.R.P.

BEYOND THE SUNSET PUBLISHER.

Westpoint, Indiana

Monday,
August 14, 2006

Part II

Department of Education

34 CFR Parts 300 and 301
Assistance to States for the Education of
Children With Disabilities and Preschool
Grants for Children With Disabilities;
Final Rule

Special Education, The Commentary: Definitions, Clarifications, and Purposes

By Patricia L. Johnson Howey, B.A., I.R.P.

Published using Dyslexie Font

Printed in the United States of America

Library of Congress Cataloging-in-Publication Data

Library of Congress Control Number: 2022901763

Johnson Howey, Patricia L

ISBN 13: 978-1-7372011-3-7

1. Education

2. Law

Using this Book

The information in this book is from the *Analysis of Comments and Changes*, typically referred to as the *Commentary*, published in the Federal Register in 2006. 71 Fed. Reg. 156, 46540-46845 (August 14, 2006). Each topic includes the Federal Register page number.

If the IDEA statute or its regulations have encoded a definition of a term, word, or phrase, generally, the author does not duplicate them here.

Every attempt has been made to ensure the accuracy of the contents. The author encourages readers to us this book is a reference and resource, but to review, refer to, and cite directly from the *Commentary*.

Some courts have used the *Commentary* to support their decisions. Included are two of these cases with citations. They are available through Google Scholar.

Since the law is not static, readers should not consider this book the final authority on definitions, clarifications, and topics found in the *Commentary*.

If an "e-book" version is published, it may include embedded links.

Monday,
August 14, 2006

Part II

Department of Education

34 CFR Parts 300 and 301
Assistance to States for the Education of
Children With Disabilities and Preschool
Grants for Children With Disabilities;
Final Rule

DEDICATION

I dedicate this book to the memory of my Saint Mary
of the Woods College academic advisor, Kathryn
Myers, whose guidance, assistance, and encourage-
ment made my college education a success.

Monday,
August 14, 2006

Part II

Department of Education

34 CFR Parts 300 and 301
Assistance to States for the Education of
Children With Disabilities and Preschool
Grants for Children With Disabilities;
Final Rule

Contents

Part II

Department of
Education

54 CFR Parts 300 and 301
Assistance to States for the Education of
Children With Disabilities and Preschool
Grants for Children With Disabilities;
Final Rule

What is the Federal Register?

The *Federal Register* is the official vehicle of the Federal government that publishes the important official government documents. It includes substantive rules and interpretations, general policy statements, descriptions of agency forms, agency promulgated rules and regulations, and many other official government documents.

When congressional bills become laws, federal departments and agencies develop proposed rules to implement the statutes. They are published in the *Federal Register* for at least 30 days. During this time, the public may comment, question, and suggest changes to the proposed rules.

The departments and agencies consider the public input at the end of the commentary period and issue a final rule. It is also published in the Federal Register.

What is the Commentary?

Congress made its last amendment to the Individuals with Disabilities Education Act (IDEA) in 2005. The U.S. Department of Education (USDOE) published its proposed rules in the Federal Register and opened the door to public comment.

On August 4, 2006, the USDOE published its *Analysis of Comments and Changes*, generally referred to as the *Commentary*, in the Federal Register. The full citation to the *Commentary* is *Assistance to States for the Education of Children With Disabilities and Preschool Grants for children With Disabilities*; *Final Rule*, 71 Fed. Reg. 156, 46540–46845 (August 14, 2006) (to be codified at 34 CFR Parts 300 and 301)

The *Commentary* summarizes the public input and explains the USDOE's reasoning as to why it did or did not make suggested changes, amendments, or edits to the proposed rules.

The *Commentary* contains definitions, clarifications, explanations, and purposes of the Regulation's words, terms, and phrases. Often, these interpretations are found *only* in the *Commentary!*

It is common for disputes and confusion to arise about the meaning of words, terms, or phrases in the Act or the regulations. The *Commentary* may have answers to questios about why the USDOE chose to use specific language in its rule or decided not to make certain changes.

While the *Commentary* is not the law, some courts have used it to support their opinions.

☞ *See: Ty v. New York Dept. of Educ.,* 584 F.3d 412 (2009) and *Sheils v. Pennsbury Sch. Dist.,* Civil Action No. 14-2736, US Dist. Ct. PA., Mem. Op. (2015)

A resource for parents, advocates, educators, attorneys, and schools, this book is a dictionary of sorts. It is designed to help readers quickly locate many words, terms, and phrases the USDOE chose to analyze in the *Commentary.* The author hopes this book will provide an efficient way to locate information in the *Commentary's* lengthy 307 pages.

CHAPTER 1: "ACADEMIC ACHIEVEMENT" TO "AUDOLOGY"

Academic Achievement

"Academic achievement generally refers to a child's performance in academic areas (e.g., reading or language arts, math, science, and history). We believe the definition could vary depending on a child's circumstance or situation, and therefore, we do not believe a definition of "academic achievement" should be included in these regulations."
p. 46662

Accommodations and Modifications

"The terms *"accommodations"* and *"modifications"* are

terms of art referring to adaptations of the educational environment, the presentation of educational material, the method of response, or the educational content. They are not, however, examples of different types of "education" and therefore we do not believe it is appropriate to define these terms of art or to include them ... §300.39(b)..."
p. 46577

Adequate Notice

"We do not think it is appropriate or necessary to include in the regulations a definition of "adequate notice" because what constitutes "adequate notice" will vary depending on the unique circumstances in each State and we believe States should have the flexibility of determining and applying a workable and reasonable standard that meets their circumstances to ensure public participation at public hearings. We believe it would be reasonable for the State to assume that it provided adequate notice if, at its public hearings, there were sufficient representatives of the general public, including individuals with disabilities and parents of children with disabilities, in attendance."
p. 46614

Agree, Agreement

"The meaning of the terms "agree" or "agreement" is not the same as consent. "Agree" or "agreement" refers to an understanding between the parent and the public agency about a particular question or issue, which may be in writing, depending on the context." p. 46551

"An agreement between a parent and a public agency is not the same as parental consent in § 300.9. Rather, an agreement refers to an understanding between a parent and the public agency and does not need to meet the requirements for parental consent in § 300.9." p. 46641

"An agreement is not the same as consent, but instead refers to an understanding between the parent and the LEA." p. 46673

 See also: Consent

All the Core Subjects

"All the core subjects" refers to the core academic subjects, which include English, reading or language arts, mathematics, science, foreign languages, civics and government, economics, arts, history, and geography, consistent with § 300.10." p. 46559

Alternate Achievement Standards

"For children under section 602(3) of the Individuals with Disabilities Education Act with the most significant cognitive disabilities who take an alternate assessment, a State may, through a documented and validated standards-setting process, define alternate academic achievement standards, provided those standards—

(1) Are aligned with the State's academic content standards;

(2) Promote access to the general curriculum; and

(3) Reflect professional judgment of the highest achievement standards possible." p. 46558

"The regulations promulgated under section 1111(b)(1) of the ESEA permit States to use alternate achievement standards to evaluate the performance of a small group of children with the most significant cognitive disabilities who are not expected to meet grade-level standards even with the best instruction. An alternate achievement standard sets an expectation of performance that differs in complexity from a grade-level achievement standard." p. 46558

"Although alternate achievement standards differ in complexity from grade-level standards, 34 CFR 200.1(d) requires that alternate achievement standards be aligned with the State's content standards, promote access to the general curriculum, and reflect professional judgment of the highest achievement standards possible." p. 46558

"The IEP Team's determination of how the child's disability affects the child's involvement and progress in the general education curriculum is a primary consideration in the development of the child's annual IEP goals. Section 300.320(a)(1)(i), consistent with section 614(d)(1)(A)(i)(I)(aa) of the Act, requires the statement of a child's present levels of performance in the IEP to include how the child's disability affects the child's involvement and progress in the general education curriculum. This directly corresponds with the provision in § 300.320(a)(2)(i)(A) and section 614(d)(1)(A)(i)(II)(aa) of the Act, which requires the IEP to include measurable annual goals designed to meet the child's needs that result from the child's disability to enable the child to be involved in and make progress in the general education curriculum. We do not believe further clarification is needed regarding the alignment of a child's present levels of performance with the child's annual goals." p. 46662

"Section 300.320(a)(2)(i), consistent with section

614(d)(1)(A)(i)(II) of the Act, requires the IEP to include measurable annual goals. Further, § 300.320(a)(3)(i), consistent with section 614(d)(1)(A)(i)(III) of the Act, requires the IEP to include a statement of how the child's progress toward meeting the annual goals will be measured. The Act does not require goals to be written for each specific discipline or to have outcomes and measures on a specific assessment tool." p. 46662

" ... [T]here is nothing in the Act that requires a child's IEP goals to be aligned with the State's alternate assessment based on alternate achievement standards. Additionally, for some children, goals may be needed for activities that are not closely related to a State's academic content and academic achievement standards." p. 46663

Alternative Means of Dispute Resolution

"ADR includes "procedures and processes that States have found to be effective in resolving disputes quickly and effectively." ADR does not include the dispute resolution processes required by the IDEA or its regulations."
p. 46604.

"We do not believe it is necessary to include in the regulations a definition of the term "alternative means of dispute resolution'' because the term is generally under-stood to refer to other procedures and processes that States have found to be effective in resolving disputes quickly and effectively but does not include those dispute resolution processes required under the Act or these final regulations.'' p. 46604

Appropriate

"The word "appropriate" in these regulations does not have a different meaning from its common usage. Generally, the word "appropriate" is used to mean "suitable" or "fit-ting" for a particular person, condition, occasion, or place." p. 46661

Appropriate Instruction

"Whether a child has received ''appropriate instruction'' is appropriately left to State and local officials to determine. Schools should have current, data-based evidence to indi-cate whether a child responds to appropriate instruction before determining that a child is a child with a disability. Children should not be identified as having a disability be-fore concluding that their performance deficits are not the result of a lack of appropriate instruction." p. 46656

Appropriate Period of Time, Reasonable Period of Time

"It is not necessary to change "appropriate period of time" to "reasonable period of time," because the terms here have similar meanings and are commonly understood to be synonymous." p. 46659

Assessments, State and Districtwide

" ... State agencies, LEAs, and schools must assess all children, regardless of whether a child is to be included for reporting or accountability purposes and regardless of the amount of time the child has been enrolled in the State agency, LEA, or school. The only public school children with disabilities enrolled in public settings who are exempted from participation in State and districtwide assessment programs under the Act are children with disabilities convicted as adults under State law and incarcerated in adult prisons (§ 300.324(d)(1)(i))." p. 46718

Assistive Technology Device

"The definition of assistive technology device in § 300.5 incorporates the definition in section 602(1)(B) of the Act ... The definition in the Act specifically refers to any item, piece of equipment, or product system that is used to increase, maintain, or improve the functional capabilities of the child and specifically excludes a medical device that is surgically implanted or the replacement of such device ... § 300.105(a) requires each public agency to ensure that assistive technology devices (or assistive technology services, or both) are made available to a child with a disability if required as part of the child's special education, related services, or supplementary aids and services. This provision ties the definition to a child's educational needs, which public agencies must meet in order to ensure that a child with a disability receives a free appropriate public education (FAPE)." p. 46547

"The definition of assistive technology device does not list specific devices, nor would it be practical or possible to include an exhaustive list of assistive technology devices. Whether an augmentative communication device, playback devices, or other devices could be considered an assistive technology device for a child depends on whether the device is used to increase, maintain, or improve the functional capabilities of a child with a disability, and whether the child's individualized education program (IEP) Team determines that the child needs the device in order to receive a free appropriate public education. However, medical devices that are surgically implanted, including those used for breathing, nutrition, and other bodily functions, are excluded from the definition of an assistive technology device in section 602(1)(B) of the Act. The exclusion applicable to a medical device that is surgically implanted includes both the implanted component of the device, as well as its external components." p. 46547

"An instructional program is not a device, and, therefore, would not meet the definition of an assistive technology device." p. 46547

"... [T]he definition of assistive technology device in §300.5 specifically excludes a medical device that is surgically implanted and the replacement of that device." p. 46548

"Section 300.5 and § 300.6 define the terms assistive technology device and assistive technology service, respectively. Section 300.105 is not part of the definition of these terms, but rather is necessary to specify the circumstances under which public agencies are responsible for making available assistive technology devices and assistive technology services to children with disabilities." p. 46581

"An assistive technology device, as defined in § 300.5, means any item, piece of equipment, or product system that is used to increase, maintain, or improve the functional capabilities of a child with a disability.

Section 602(1) of the Act clarifies that the definition of assistive technology device does not include a medical device that is surgically implanted or the replacement of such device. Section 602(26) of the Act also stipulates that only medical services that are for diagnostic and evaluative purposes and required to assist a child with a disability to benefit from special education are considered a related service. We believe Congress was clear in its intent in S. Rpt. 108–185, p. 8, which states:

> [T]he definitions of "assistive technology device" and "related services" do not include a medical device that is surgically implanted, or the post-surgical maintenance, programming, or replacement of such device, or an external device connected with the use of a surgically implanted medical device (other than the costs of performing routine maintenance and monitoring of such external device at the same time the child is receiving other services under the act).

The Department believes, however, that public agencies have an obligation to change a battery or routinely check an external component of a surgically implanted medical device to make sure it is turned on and operating.

However, mapping a cochlear implant (or paying the costs associated with mapping) is not routine checking as described above and should not be the responsibility of a public agency." pp. 46581–46582

 See also: Assistive Technology Service

Assistive Technology Program, State Agency Responsibility

"Section 300.172(d) and section 612(a)(23)(D) of the Act provide that in carrying out the requirements in § 300.172, the SEA, to the maximum extent possible, must work collaboratively with the State agency responsible for assistive technology programs. Section 612(a)(23)(D) of the Act does not refer to any particular assistive technology program. Therefore, we interpret broadly the phrase "State agency responsible for assistive technology programs" to mean the agency determined by the State to be responsible for assistive technology programs, which may include programs established under section 4 of the Assistive Technology Act of 1998, as amended." p. 46621

Assistive Technology Service

" ... [T]he definition is clear that an assistive technology service is any service that helps a child with a disability select an appropriate assistive technology device, obtain the device, or train the child to use the device." p. 46548

"The definition of *assistive technology service* does not list specific services. We do not believe it is practical or possible to include an exhaustive list of assistive technology services ..." p. 46548

 See also: Assistive Technology Device

At No Cost

"The term **FAPE** is defined in § 300.17 and section 602(9)(D) of the Act as including, among other elements, special education and related services, provided at no cost to parents, in conformity with an individualized education program (IEP)." p. 46580

"FAPE includes not just the special education and related services that a child with a disability receives, but also includes an appropriate preschool, elementary and secondary school education in the State involved. The required special education and related services must be provided at public expense, at no cost to the parent, in accordance with an **IEP**, and the education provided to the child must meet the standards that apply to educational services provided by the **SEA** and **LEA** (except for the highly qualified teacher requirements in §§ 300.18 and 300.156(c))." p. 46598

"Section 300.306(a)(2), consistent with section 614(b)(4)(B) of the Act, requires that a copy of the evaluation report and the documentation of determination of eligibility be given to the parent ... at no cost." p. 46656

"[T]he public agency must provide a copy of an evaluation report and the documentation of determination of eligibility at no cost to the parent." p. 46678

"... Section 300.322(f) ... requires the public agency to give the parent a copy of the child's IEP at no cost to the parent. p. 46687.

Attorneys' Fees

"The awarding of attorneys' fees is not addressed in §300.151(b) because the State complaint process is not an administrative proceeding or judicial action, and, therefore, the awarding of attorneys' fees is not available under the Act for State complaint resolutions." p. 46602

"Section 300.517(c)(2)(iii) of the regulations, consistent with section 615(i)(3)(D)(iii) of the Act, specifies that the resolution meeting is not considered to be a meeting convened as a result of an administrative hearing or judicial action or an administrative hearing or judicial action for purposes of the attorneys' fees provision. Accordingly, such fees may not be awarded for resolution meetings.

While it is clear that attorneys' fees may not be awarded for resolution meetings, the Act is silent as to whether attorneys' fees are available for activities that occur outside the resolution meeting conducted pursuant to section 615(f)(1)(B)(i) of the Act and § 300.510(a). We decline to regulate on this issue because we believe these determinations will be fact-specific and should be left to the discretion of the court." p. 46708

"Although we have no reliable data on average attorneys' fees in due process cases, for purposes of this analysis, the Department assumes an hourly rate of $300 as an upper limit. The Department further assumes that each instance in which a party chooses to hire an attorney sooner as a result of this change will involve no more than three additional hours of work." p. 46748

"Section 615(i)(3)(B) of the Act allows a court to award reasonable attorneys' fees as a part of the costs to a parent who is the prevailing party. Although the Act also provides parents with the right to be accompanied and advised by individuals with special knowledge or training with respect to the problems of children with disabilities at a due process hearing, it does not provide for awarding attorneys' fees to these other individuals. Lay advocates are, by definition, not attorneys and are not entitled to compensation as if they were attorneys." p. 466708

Audiology

"The term audiology, as defined in § 300.34(c)(1), focuses on identifying and serving children who are deaf or hard of hearing." p. 46571

CHAPTER 2: "BEHAVIOR" TO "CULTURAL"

Behavior, Behavior Intervention Plans

"We ... recognize ... that as a matter of practice, it makes a great deal of sense to attend to behavior of children with disabilities that is interfering with their education or that of others, so that the behavior can be addressed, even when that behavior will not result in a change in placement. In fact, the Act emphasizes a proactive approach to behaviors that interfere with learning by requiring that, for children with disabilities whose behavior impedes their learning or that of others, the IEP Team consider, as appropriate, and address in the child's IEP, "the use of positive behavioral interventions, and other strategies to address the behavior." (See section 614(d)(3)(B)(i) of the Act). This provision should ensure that children who need behavior intervention plans to succeed in school receive them." p. 46721

Career-Technical

 See also: Vocational Education

Charter School

" ... [W]e are including the current definition of charter school in section 5210(1) of the **ESEA** here for reference. The term charter school means a public school that:

1) In accordance with a specific State statute authorizing the granting of charters to schools, is exempt from significant State or local rules that inhibit the flexible operation and management of public schools, but not from any rules relating to the other requirements of this paragraph [the paragraph that sets forth the Federal definition];

2) Is created by a developer as a public school, or is adapted by a developer from an existing public school, and is operated under public supervision and direction;

3) Operates in pursuit of a specific set of educational objectives determined by the school's developer and agreed to by the authorized public chartering agency;

4) Provides a program of elementary or secondary education, or both;

5) Is nonsectarian in its programs, admissions policies, employment practices, and all other operations, and is not affiliated with a sectarian school or religious institution;

6) Does not charge tuition;

7) Complies with the Age Discrimination Act of 1975, Title VI of the Civil Rights Act of 1964, Title IX of the Education Amendments of 1972, Section 504 of the Rehabilitation Act of 1973, Title II of the Americans with Disabilities Act of 1990, and Part B of the Individuals with Disabilities Education Act;

8) Is a school to which parents choose to send their children, and that admits students on the basis of a lottery, if more students apply for admission than can be accommodated;

9) Agrees to comply with the same Federal and State audit requirements as do other elementary schools and secondary schools in the State, unless such requirements are specifically waived for the purpose of this program [the Public Charter School Program];

10) Meets all applicable Federal, State, and local health

and safety requirements;

11) Operates in accordance with State law; and

12) Has a written performance contract with the authorized public chartering agency in the State that includes a description of how student performance will be measured in charter schools pursuant to State assessments that are required of other schools and pursuant to any other assessments mutually agreeable to the authorized public chartering agency and the charter school." p. 46548

"For purposes of the Act, the definitions of charter school, elementary school, and secondary school in §§ 300.7, 300.13, and 300.36, respectively, require that a public elementary or secondary charter school be a nonprofit entity. Therefore, a public elementary or secondary charter school established as its own LEA under State law, also must be a nonprofit entity. Although these regulations do not specifically define nonprofit, the definition in 34 CFR § 77.1 applies to these regulations." p. 46565

Child Count

"The purpose of the child count under § 300.132(c) is to determine the amount of Federal funds that the LEA must spend on providing special education and related services to parentally-placed private school children with disabilities in the next fiscal year." p. 46594

Child Find, Part B and Part C

"The child find requirements in §300.111 have traditionally been interpreted to mean identifying and evaluating children beginning at birth. While child find under Part C of the Act overlaps, in part, with child find under Part B of the Act, the coordination of child find activities under Part B and Part C is an implementation matter that is best left to each State. Nothing in the Act or these regulations prohibits a Part C lead agency's participation, with the agreement of the SEA, in the actual implementation of child find activities for infants and toddlers with disabilities." p. 46584

"We also believe it is important to clarify that a child suspected of having a disability but who has not failed, is making academic progress, and is passing from grade to grade must be considered in the child find process as any other child suspected of having a disability. ... [C]hildren do not have to fail or be retained in a course or grade in order to be considered for special education and related services." p. 46584.

"We recognize that it is difficult to locate, identify, and evaluate highly mobile and migrant children with disabilities. However, we strongly believe it is important to stress in these regulations that the States' child find responsibilities in § 300.111 apply eaually to such children." p. 46584

"Homeless children are ... included in the child find reauirements. Section 300.111(a)(1)(i) clarifies that the State must have policies and procedures to ensure that children with disabilities who are homeless and who are in need of special education and related services, are identified, located, and evaluated". p. 46584

"We believe §300.111(a), consistent with section 612(a)(3)(A) of the Act, clarifies that the State must ensure that all children with disabilities residing in the State are identified, located, and evaluated. This would include children in residential facilities." pp. 46584-46585

"Section 612(a)(10)(A)(i)(II) of the Act provides that the LEA where the private elementary schools and secondary schools are located, after timely and meaningful consultation with private school representatives, is responsible for conducting the child find process to determine the number of parentally-placed children with disabilities attending private schools located in the LEA. We believe this responsibility includes child find for children who reside in other States but who attend private elementary schools and secondary schools located in the LEA, because section 612(a)(10)(A)(i)(II) of the Act is clear about which LEA is responsible for child find and the Act does not provide an exception for children who reside in one State and attend private elementary schools and secondary schools in other States." p. 46591.

"If a private preschool or day care program is considered an elementary school, as defined in §300.13, the *child find* and equitable services participation requirements in §§ 300.130 through 300.144, consistent with section 612(a)(10) of the Act, apply to children with disabilities aged three through five enrolled by their parents in such programs." p. 46591

"Under section 612(a)(10)(A) of the Act, the obligation to conduct child find and provide equitable services extends to children who are enrolled by their parents in private elementary schools and secondary schools. This obligation also applies to children who have been enrolled by their parents in private facilities if those facilities are elementary schools or secondary schools, as defined in subpart A of the regulations." p. 46591

"The LEA where the private elementary schools and secondary schools are located must identify and evaluate all children suspected of having disabilities as defined under section 602(3) of the Act. LEAs may not exclude children suspected of having certain disabilities, such as those with specific learning disabilities, from their child find activities. The Department recommends that LEAs and private elementary schools and secondary schools consult on how best to implement the State's evaluation criteria and the requirements under this part for identifying children with specific learning disabilities enrolled in private schools by their parents." p. 46592

"Section 300.131(c), consistent with section 612(a)(10)(A)(ii)(III) of the Act, requires that, in carrying out child find for parentally-placed private school children, SEAs and LEAs must undertake activities similar to those activities undertaken for their publicly enrolled or publicly-placed children. This would generally include, but is not limited to, such activities as widely distributing informational brochures, providing regular public service announcements, staffing exhibits at health fairs and other community activities, and creating direct liaisons with private schools. Activities for child find must be completed in a time period comparable to those activities for public school children. This means that LEAs must conduct child find activities, including individual evaluations, for parentally-placed private school children within a reasonable period of time and without undue delay, and may not wait until after child find for public school children is conducted. In addition, evaluations of all children suspected of having disabilities under Part B of the Act, regardless of whether they are enrolled by their parents in private elementary schools or secondary schools, must be conducted in accordance with the requirements in §§ 300.300 through 300.311, consistent with section 614(a) through (c) of the Act, which describes the procedures for evaluations and reevaluations for all children with disabilities." p. 46593.

"Child find ... is a part of the basic obligation that public agencies have to all children with disabilities, and failure to locate, identify, and evaluate a parentally-placed private school child would be subject to due process. Therefore, the due process provisions in §§ 300.504 through 300.519 do apply to complaints that the LEA where the private school is located failed to meet the consent and evaluation requirements in §§ 300.300 through 311."
p. 46597

"Child find activities typically involve some sort of

screening process to determine whether the child should be referred for a full evaluation to determine eligibility for special education and related services." p. 46636

 See also: Screening

"The child find requirements permit referrals from any source that suspects a child may be eligible for special education and related services." p. 46636

"The *child find* requirements in § 300.111 and section 612(a)(3)(A) of the Act require that all children with disabilities in the State who are in need of special education and related services be identified, located, and evaluated. Therefore, it would generally not be acceptable for an **LEA** to wait several months to conduct an evaluation or to seek parental consent for an initial evaluation if the public agency suspects the child to be a child with a disability." p. 46637

Child, Child with a Disability, Student

"... [I]f a child has one of the disabilities listed in §300.8(a)(2)(i), but only needs a related service, the child is not a child with a disability under the Act. However, §300.8(a)(2)(ii) provides that, if a State considers a particular service that could be encompassed by the definition of *related services* also to be special education, then the child would be determined to be a child with a disability under the Act." p. 46549

" ... [A]a child does not have to fail or be retained in a course or grade in order to be considered for special education and related services. However, in order to be a child with a disability under the Act, a child must have one or more of the impairments identified in section 602(3) of the Act and need special education and related services because of that impairment." p. 46549

"A child would not be considered a child with a disability under the Act if the child has not been evaluated in accordance with §§ 300.301 through 300.311 and determined to have one of the disabilities in § 300.8(a), and because of that disability, needs special education and related services." p. 46632

"A child who is at risk for having any disability under the Act is not considered a child with a disability under §300.8 and section 602(3) of the Act and, therefore, is not eligible for services under the Act." p. 46550

"The words "child" and "student" are used interchangeably throughout the Act. The regulations follow the statutory language whenever possible. In § 300.320, we used the term "child with a disability," consistent with section 614(d) of the Act." p. 46661

"The Act does not require children to be identified with a particular disability category for purposes of the delivery of special education and related services. In other words, while the Act requires that the Department collect aggregate data on children's disabilities, it does not require that particular children be labeled with particular disabilities for purposes of service delivery, since a child's entitlement under the Act is to FAPE and not to a particular disability label." p. 46737

Child with a Disability, BIA- Funded School, Incarcerated in State Prison

"As a general matter, for educational purposes, students who were enrolled in a BIA-funded school and are subsequently convicted as an adult and incarcerated in a State run adult prison are the responsibility of the State where the adult prison is located. Section 612(a)(11)(C) of the Act and § 300.149(d) allow flexibility to States in that the Governor, or another individual pursuant to State law, can designate a public agency in the State, other than the SEA, as responsible for ensuring that FAPE is made

available to eligible students with disabilities who are convicted under State law and incarcerated in the State's
adult prisons. This provision does not apply to the Secretary of the Interior. Therefore, the Office of Indian Education Programs cannot delegate the responsibility of ensuring that the requirements of Part B of the Act are met by
the State prison. The Act does not specifically address
who is responsible for education of students with disabilities in tribally controlled detention facilities. However, the
Secretary of the Interior is only responsible for students
who are enrolled in schools operated or funded by the Department of the Interior." p. 46600

Child, High Need

"Section 300.704(c)(3)(i)(A), consistent with section
611(e)(3)(C)(i) of the Act, requires the SEA to establish a
State definition of a high need child with a disability in
consultation with LEAs. The Act does not require the involvement of parents, representatives of the State Advisory panel, or other stakeholders. However, there is nothing in the Act or these regulations that would prohibit a
State from consulting with these or other groups, if the
State chooses to do so." p. 46741

Child with Mental Retardation

"Section 602(3)(A) of the Act refers to a "child with mental retardation," not a "child with intellectual disabilities," and we do not see a compelling reason to change the term. However, States are free to use a different term to refer to a child with mental retardation, as long as all children who would be eligible for special education and related services under the Federal definition of *mental retardation* receive FAPE." p. 46550

Cochlear Implant Mapping and Optimization

"The term "mapping" refers to the optimization of a cochlear implant and is not included in the definition of related services. Specifically, "mapping" and "optimization" refer to adjusting the electrical stimulation levels provided by the cochlear implant that is necessary for long-term post-surgical follow-up of a cochlear implant." p. 46569

"Optimization" or "mapping" adjusts or fine tunes the electrical stimulation levels provided by the cochlear implant and is changed as a child learns to discriminate signals to a finer degree. Optimization services are generally provided at a specialized clinic." p. 46570

"A cochlear implant is an electronic device surgically

implanted to stimulate nerve endings in the inner ear (cochlea) in order to receive and process sound and speech. The device has two parts, one that is surgically implanted and attached to the skull and, the second, an externally worn speech processor that attaches to a port in the implant. The internal device is intended to be permanent." p. 46570

"Optimization generally refers to the mapping necessary to make the cochlear implant work properly and involves adjusting the electrical stimulation levels provided by the cochlear implant." p. 46570

" ... "[W]e believe it is important to clarify that a public agency is responsible for the routine checking of the external components of a surgically implanted device in much the same manner as a public agency is responsible for the proper functioning of hearing aids." p. 46571

Comparable

"We do not believe it is necessary to define "comparable services" in these regulations because the Department interprets "comparable" to have the plain meaning of the word, which is "similar" or "equivalent." Therefore, when used with respect to a child who transfers to a new public agency from a previous public agency in the same State (or from another State), "comparable" services means services that are "similar" or "equivalent" to those that were described in the child's IEP from the previous public agency, as determined by the child's newly designated IEP Team in the new public agency." p. 46681

Competent Authority

"Competent authority is defined in 36 CFR 701.6(b)(2) as follows: (i) In cases of blindness, visual disability, or physical limitations "competent authority" is defined to include doctors of medicine, doctors of osteopathy, ophthalmologists, optometrists, registered nurses, therapists, professional staff of hospitals, institutions, and public or welfare agencies (e.g., social workers, case workers, counselors, rehabilitation teachers, and superintendents). (ii) In the case of a reading disability from organic dysfunction, competent authority is defined as doctors of medicine who may consult with colleagues in associated disciplines." p. 46621

Complaints, Due Process

"While there may be legitimate issues regarding the provision of services to a particular parentally-placed private school child with a disability an LEA has agreed to serve, the due process provisions in section 615 of the Act and §§ 300.504 through 300.519 do not apply to these disputes, because there is no individual right to these services under the Act. Disputes that arise about these services are properly subject to the State complaint procedures under §§ 300.151 through 300.153." p. 46597

" ... [P]arents of parentally-placed private school children with disabilities may file a due process complaint with the LEA in which the private school is located (and forward a copy to the SEA) regarding an LEA's failure to meet the consent and evaluation requirements in §§ 300.300 through 300.311." p. 46597

Complaints, State

"We do not believe it is necessary to clarify in the regulations that the State complaint procedures can be used to resolve a complaint regarding the denial of appropriate services or FAPE for a child, since § 300.153 is sufficiently clear that an organization or individual may file a written complaint that a public agency has violated a requirement of Part B of the Act or part 300. The State complaint procedures can be used to resolve any complaint that meets the requirements of § 300.153, including matters concerning the identification, evaluation, or educational placement of the child, or the provision of FAPE to the child." p. 46601

"It is important to clarify that when the parent files both a due process complaint and a State complaint on the same issue, the State must set aside any part of the complaint that is being addressed in the due process hearing until the conclusion of the hearing. However, any issue in the complaint that is not a part of the due process hearing must be resolved using the State complaint procedures in § 300.152, including using the time limit and procedures in paragraphs (b) and (d) of § 300.152. (See § 300.152(c)(1)). Under the Act, the decision reached through the due process proceedings is the final decision on those matters, unless a party to the hearing appeals that decision by requesting State-level review, if applicable, or by bringing a civil action in an appropriate State or Federal court."
p. 46601

"The SEA is responsible for ensuring that all public agencies within its jurisdiction meet the requirements of the Act and its implementing regulations. In light of the SEA's general supervisory authority and responsibility under sections 612(a)(11) and 616 of the Act, we believe the SEA should have broad flexibility to determine the appropriate remedy or corrective action necessary to resolve a complaint in which the **SEA** has found that the public agency has failed to provide appropriate services to children with disabilities, including awarding monetary reimbursement and compensatory services." p. 46602

" ...The **State** complaint process is intended to be less adversarial than the more formal filing of a due process complaint and possibly going to a due process hearing ..." p. 46605

"The purpose of requiring the party filing the complaint to forward a copy of the complaint to the **LEA** or public agency serving the child, at the same time the party files the complaint with the **SEA**, is to ensure that the public agency involved has knowledge of the issues and an opportunity to resolve them directly with the complaining party at the earliest possible time. The sooner the **LEA** knows that a complaint is filed and the nature of the issue(s), the quicker the **LEA** can work directly with the complainant to resolve the complaint. We believe the benefit of having the complainant forward a copy of the complaint to the **LEA** or public agency far outweigh the minimal burden placed on the complainant because it will lead to a faster resolution of the complaint at the local level. For these reasons, we also do not believe it is more efficient to have the **SEA** forward the complaint to the public agency or provide the public agency with a statement summarizing the complaint." p. 46606

 See also: Complaints, Due Process

Complaints, State, Complainant Confidentiality

"We do not believe that the complaint procedures should provide for the confidentiality of the complainant. The complainant should not remain unknown to the public agency that is the subject of the complaint because that public agency needs to know who the complainant is and something about the complaint (consistent with § 300.153) before it can be expected to resolve the issues. We believe it is reasonable to require a party to file a signed complaint and provide contact information to the SEA in order to ensure the credibility of the complaint and provide the SEA with the basic contact information necessary for the SEA to handle complaints expeditiously. If the SEA receives a complaint that is not signed, as required in § 300.153, the SEA may choose to dismiss the complaint." p. 46606

Complaints, State, Consent

"We do not agree that *consent*, as defined in § 300.9,

should be required to extend the 60-day time limit because it would add burden and is not necessary. It is sufficient to require agreement of the parties. p. 46604

Complaints, State, Statute of Limitations

"Limiting a complaint to a violation that occurred not more than one year prior to the date that the complaint is received will help ensure that problems are raised and addressed promptly so that children receive **FAPE**." 46606

Consent

"These terms are used throughout the regulations and are consistent with their use in the Act. The definition of consent requires a parent to be fully informed of all information relevant to the activity for which consent is sought. The definition also requires a parent to agree in writing to an activity for which consent is sought. Therefore, whenever consent is used in these regulations, it means that the consent is both informed and in writing." p. 46551

"The definition of consent already requires that the parent be fully informed of all the information relevant to the activity for which consent is sought." p. 46551

"We believe obtaining parental consent each time the public agency seeks to use a parent's *public* insurance or other public benefits to provide or pay for a service is important to protect the privacy rights of the parent and to ensure that the parent is fully informed of a public agency's access to his or her public benefits or insurance and the services paid by the public benefits or insurance program ... parental consent is required each time the public agency seeks to use the parent's *public* insurance or other public benefits ... a public agency could satisfy parental consent requirements under **FERPA** and section 617(c) of the Act if the parent provided the required parental consent to the **State** Medicaid agency, and the consent satisfied the Part **B** definition of *consent* in § 300.9." p. 46608

"The definition of *consent* in § 300.9 includes the requirement that a parent be fully informed of all information relevant to the activity for which consent is sought. The definition also requires that a parent agree in writing to carrying out the activity for which the parent's consent is sought. Therefore, whenever the term "consent" is used in these regulations, it means that the consent is both "informed" and "written." Similarly, the terms "consent," "informed consent," "parental consent," and "written informed consent," as used in these regulations, all are intended to have the same meaning." p. 46629

"Consent under § 300.9(b) requires a parent to understand and agree in writing to the carrying out of the activity for which the parent's consent is sought." p. 46629

"*Consent*, as defined in § 300.9, means that the parent has been fully informed in his or her native language, or other mode of communication, and understands and agrees *in writing* to the initial evaluation." p. 46632

Consultation Services

"The definition of consultation services and whether a special education teacher provides consultation services are matters best left to the discretion of each State." p. 46558

Co-Teaching

"The term "co-teaching" has many different meanings depending on the context in which it is used. Whether and how co-teaching is implemented is a matter that is best left to State and local officials' discretion." p. 46561

Core Academic Subjects

"The definition of core academic subjects in § 300.10, consistent with section 602(4) of the Act, is the same as the definition in section 9101 of the ESEA ... However, there is nothing in the Act or these regulations that would prevent a State from including additional subjects in its definition of "core academic subjects." p. 46552

"The definition of core academic subjects does not vary for secondary students who are functioning significantly below grade level. The Act focuses on high academic standards and clear performance goals for children with disabilities that are consistent with the standards and expectations for all children. As required in § 300.320(a), each child's IEP must include annual goals to enable the child to be involved in and make progress in the general education curriculum, and a statement of the special education and related services and supplementary aids and services to enable the child to be involved and make progress in the general education curriculum." p. 46552

" ... [T]he ESEA does not identify "social sciences" as a core academic subject. Neither does it identify "social studies" as a core academic subject. Instead, it identifies specific core academic areas: History, geography, economics, and civics and government." p. 46552

Cultural

"We believe the term "cultural" is generally understood and do not see a need for further clarification." p. 46551

Part II

Department of
Education

34 CFR Parts 300 and 301
Assistance to States for the Education of
Children With Disabilities and Preschool
Grants for Children With Disabilities;
Final Rule

August 14, 2006

CHAPTER 3: "DANGEROUS WEAPON" TO "EDUCATIONAL RECORDS"

Dangerous Weapon

"The term *dangerous weapon means* a weapon, device, instrument, material, or substance, animate or inanimate, that is used for, or is readily capable of, causing death or serious bodily injury, except that such term does not include a pocket knife with a blade of less than 2 1/2 inches in length." (Section 930(g)(2) of title 18, USC) p. 46723

Data-Based Documentation

"Data-based documentation" refers to an objective and systematic process of documenting a child's progress. This type of assessment is a feature of strong instruction in reading and math and is consistent with § 300.306(b)(1)(i) and (ii) and section 614(b)(5)(A) and (B) of the Act, that children cannot be identified for special education if an achievement problem is due to lack of appropriate instruction in reading or math." p. 46657

Day, Business Day, School Day

"School day, as defined in § 300.11(c)(1), is any day or partial day that children are in attendance at school for instructional purposes. If children attend school for only part of a school day and are released early (e.g., on the last day before summer vacation), that day would be considered to be a school day." p. 46552

"Section 300.11(c)(2) ... defines school day as having the same meaning for all children, including children with and without disabilities. Therefore, it is unnecessary for the regulations to clarify that non-instructional time (e.g., recess, lunch) is not counted as instructional time for a child with a disability unless such times are counted as instructional time for all children. Consistent with this requirement, days on which ESY services are provided cannot be counted as a school day because ESY services are provided only to children with disabilities." p. 46552

Deaf or Hard of Hearing

"[Section] 300.324(a)(2)(iv), consistent with section 614(d)(3)(B)(iv) of the Act, clarifies that the IEP Team, in developing the IEP for a child who is deaf or hard of hearing, must consider the child's language and communication needs, opportunities for direct communication with peers and professional personnel in the child's language and communication mode, and the child's academic level and full range of needs, including opportunities for direct instruction in the child's language and communication mode." p. 46586

Developmental Delay

"Section 300.8(b) states that the use of the developmental delay category for a child with a disability aged three through nine, or any subset of that age range, must be made in accordance with § 300.111(b). Section 300.111(b) gives States the option of adopting a definition of developmental delay, but does not require an LEA to adopt and use the term. However, if an LEA uses the category of developmental delay, the LEA must conform to both the State's definition of the term and the age range that has been adopted by the State. If a State does not adopt the category of developmental delay, an LEA may not use that category as the basis for establishing a child's eligibility for special education and related services." p. 46549

"[A] child does not have to fail or be retained in a course or grade in order to be considered for special education and related services. However, in order to be a child with a disability under the Act, a child must have one or more of the impairments identified in section 602(3) of the Act and need special education and related services because of that impairment." p. 46549

Discrepancy Models

"Discrepancy models are not essential for identifying children with SLD who are gifted. However, the regulations clearly allow discrepancies in achievement domains, typical of children with SLD who are gifted, to be used to identify children with SLD." p. 46647

Disciplinary School Removals

"The Department has long interpreted the Act to permit schools to remove a child with a disability who violates a code of student conduct from his or her current placement for not more than 10 consecutive school days, and that additional removals of 10 consecutive school days or less in the same school year would be possible, as long as those removals do not constitute a change in placement. The requirements in § 300.530(b) do not permit using repeated disciplinary removals of 10 school days or less as a means of avoiding the change in placement options in §300.536. We believe it is important for purposes of school safety and order to preserve the authority that school personnel have to be able to remove a child for a discipline infraction for a short period of time, even though the child already may have been removed for more than 10 school days in that school year, as long as the pattern of removals does not itself constitute a change in placement of the child.

On the other hand, discipline must not be used as a means of disconnecting a child with a disability from education. Section 300.530(d) clarifies, in general, that the child must continue to receive educational services so that the child can continue to participate in the general curriculum (although in another setting), and progress toward meeting the goals in the child's IEP." p. 46715

"Section 300.530(d) clarifies that decisions regarding the extent to which services would need to be provided and the amount of services that would be necessary to enable a child with a disability to appropriately participate in the general curriculum and progress toward achieving the goals on the child's IEP may be different if the child is removed from his or her regular placement for a short period of time. For example, a child who is removed for a short period of time and who is performing at grade level may not need the same kind and amount of services to meet this standard as a child who is removed from his or her regular placement for 45 days under § 300.530(g) or § 300.532 and not performing at grade level." p. 46716

"We caution that we do not interpret "participate" to mean that a school or district must replicate every aspect of the services that a child would receive if in his or her normal classroom. For example, it would not generally be feasible for a child removed for disciplinary reasons to receive every aspect of the services that a child would receive if in his or her chemistry or auto mechanics classroom as these classes generally are taught using a hands-on component or specialized equipment or facilities." p. 46716

" ... [W]e read the Act as modifying the concept of FAPE in circumstances where a child is removed from his or her current placement for disciplinary reasons. Specifically, we interpret section 615(k)(1)(D)(i) of the Act to require that the special education and related services that are necessary to enable the child to continue to participate in the general education curriculum and to progress toward meeting the goals set out in the child's IEP, must be provided at public expense, under public supervision and direction, and, to the extent appropriate to the circumstances, be provided in conformity with the child's IEP." p. 46716

 See also: "Manifestation Determination," "Unique Circumstances"

Dispute Resolution Training

"There is nothing in the Act that would prevent a public agency from offering training in dispute resolution or referring parents to organizations that provide training in dispute resolution. Such matters are best left to local and State officials to determine, based on the training needs of parents and families." p. 46701

Due Process Hearing, Expedited

" ... [O]ne purpose of the expedited hearing is to provide protection to the child." p. 46726

" ... [W]hile a State may establish different State imposed procedural rules for expedited due process hearings conducted under this section than it has established for other due process hearings, the State must ensure that the requirements in §§ 300.510 through 300.514 are met. This will ensure that the basic protections regarding expedited hearings under the Act are met, while enabling States, in light of the expedited nature of these hearings, to adjust other procedural rules they have established for due process hearings." p. 46726

Early Intervening Services

"We believe that § 300.226(c), which states that nothing in § 300.226 will be construed to delay appropriate evaluation of a child suspected of having a disability, makes clear that early intervening services may not delay an appropriate evaluation of a child suspected of having a disability." p. 46626

"Children receiving early intervening services do not have the same rights and protections as children identified as eligible for services under sections 614 and 615 of the Act. Section 300.226(c), consistent with section 613(f)(3) of the Act, is clear that early intervening services neither limit nor create a right to FAPE." p. 46626

"We do not believe it is appropriate or necessary to

specify how long a child can receive early intervening services before an initial evaluation is conducted. If a child receiving early intervening services is suspected of having a disability, the LEA must conduct a full and individual evaluation in accordance with §§ 300.301, 300.304 and 300.305 to determine if the child is a child with a disability and needs special education and related services." p. 46626

"A child previously identified as being a child with a disability who currently does not need special education or related services would not be prevented from receiving early intervening services. For example, a child who received special education services in kindergarten and had services discontinued in grade 1 (because the public agency and the parent agreed that the child was no longer a child with a disability), could receive early intervening services in grade 2 if the child was found to be in need of additional academic and behavioral supports to succeed in the general education environment." p. 46626

"Section 613(f)(1) of the Act generally permits LEAs to use funds for early intervening services for children in kindergarten through grade 12 (with a particular emphasis on children in kindergarten through grade 3) who have not been identified as needing special education or related services, but who need additional academic and behavioral support to succeed in a general education environment. No other restrictions on this authority, such as a requirement that the LEA first demonstrate that it is providing FAPE to all eligible children, are specified or appropriate. The authority to use some Part B funds for early intervening services has the potential to benefit special education, as well as the education of other children, by reducing academic and behavioral problems in the regular educational environment and reducing the number of referrals to special education that could have been avoided by relatively simple regular education interventions. Therefore, we believe the use of Part B funds for early intervening services should be encouraged, rather than restricted." pp. 46626–46627

"In one instance, however, the Act requires the use of funds for early intervening services. Under section 618(d)(2)(B) of the Act, LEAs that are identified as having significant disproportionality based on race and ethnicity with respect to the identification of children with disabilities, the placement of children with disabilities in particular educational settings, and the incidence, duration, and type of disciplinary actions taken against children with disabilities, including suspensions and expulsions, are required to reserve the maximum amount of funds under section

613(f)(1) of the Act to provide early intervening services to children in the LEA, particularly to children in those groups that were significantly over-identified. This requirement is in recognition of the fact that significant disproportionality in special education may be the result of inappropriate regular education responses to academic or behavioral issues." p. 46627

"There is nothing in the Act that would preclude LEAs from using Part B funds for early intervening services, including literacy instruction, that target at-risk limited English proficient students who have not been identified as needing special education or related services, but who need additional academic and behavioral support to succeed in a general education environment." p. 46627

"...[S]ection 300.226, consistent with section 613(f) of the Act, states that LEAs may use Part B funds to develop and implement coordinated early intervening services." p. 46627

"Early intervening services may not be used for preschool children. Section 300.226(a) tracks the statutory language in section 613(f)(1) of the Act, which states that early intervening services are for children in kindergarten through grade 12, with a particular emphasis on children in kindergarten through grade 3." p. 46627

"Early intervening services provided under section 613(f) of the Act are services for children in kindergarten through grade 12 (with a particular emphasis on children in kindergarten through grade 3) who have not been identified as needing special education and related services, but who need additional academic and behavioral support to succeed in a general education environment.

Early intervention services, on the other hand, are services for children birth through age two that are designed to meet the developmental needs of infants and toddlers with disabilities under section 632 in Part C of the Act. Section 632(5)(A) of the Act defines infant or toddler with a disability as a child under the age of three years who (a) is experiencing developmental delays in one or more of the areas of cognitive development, physical development, communication development, social or emotional development, and adaptive development, or (b) has a diagnosed physical or mental condition that has a high probability of resulting in developmental delay. In addition, some States also provide early intervention services to infants and toddlers who are at risk of having a developmental delay. The Part C regulations will address, in detail, the early intervention services provided under section 632 of the Act." p. 46627

"Section 300.226(b) follows the specific language in section 613(f)(2) of the Act and requires that in implementing co-ordinated, early intervening services, an **LEA** may provide, among other services, professional development for teachers and other personnel to enable such personnel to deliver scientifically based academic and behavioral interventions." p. 46627

 See also: Scientifically based research.

"State and local officials are in the best position to make decisions regarding the provision of early intervening services, including the specific personnel to provide the services and the instructional materials and approaches to be used. Nothing in the Act or regulations prevents States and **LEAs** from including related services personnel in the development and delivery of educational and behavioral evaluations, services, and supports for teachers and other school staff to enable them to deliver coordinated, early intervening services." pp. 46627–46628

"Section 300.226, consistent with section 613(f) of the Act, gives **LEAs** flexibility to develop and implement coordinated, early intervening services for children who are not currently receiving special education services, but who require additional academic and behavioral support to succeed in a regular education environment. Early intervening services will benefit both the regular and special education programs by reducing academic and behavioral problems in the regular education program and the number of inappropriate referrals for special education and related services." p. 46628

"... [S]upplemental instructional materials may be used, where appropriate, to support early intervening activities. The Conf. Rpt. in note 269 provides that

> [E]arly intervening services should make use of supplemental instructional materials, where appropriate, to support student learning. Children targeted for early intervening services under IDEA are the very students who are most likely to need additional reinforcement to the core curriculum used in the regular classroom. These are in fact the additional instructional materials that have been developed to supplement and therefore strengthen the efficacy of comprehensive core curriculum."

p. 46628

"...[T]he terms "services" and "supports" in §300.226(b)(2) are broad enough to include the use of supplemental instructional materials. Accordingly, we believe that it is unnecessary to add further clarification regarding the use of supplemental instructional materials in § 300.226. Of course, use of funds for this purpose is subject to other requirements that apply to any use of funds, such as the limitation on purchase of equipment in section 605 of the Act and applicable requirements in 34 CFR Parts 76 and 80." p. 46628

"Section 300.226, consistent with section 613(f) of the Act, gives LEAs flexibility to develop and implement coordinated, early intervening services for children who are not currently receiving special education services, but who require additional academic and behavioral support to succeed in a regular education environment. Early intervening services will benefit both the regular and special education programs by reducing academic and behavioral problems in the regular education program and the number of inappropriate referrals for special education and related services." p. 46628

"Section 300.226(d), consistent with section 613(f)(4) of the Act, requires LEAs that develop and maintain coordinated, early intervening services to annually report to their SEA on the number of children receiving early intervening services and the number of those children who eventually are identified as children with disabilities and receive special education and related services during the preceding two year period (i.e., the two years after the child has received early intervening services." p. 46628

"The Department intends for LEAs to report on children who began receiving special education services no more than two years after they received early intervening services. For the preceding two year period, the LEA would report on the number of children who received both early intervening services and special education services during those two years." p. 46628

Early Intervening Services, Preschool

"Early intervening services may not be used for preschool children. Section 300.226(a) tracks the statutory language in section 613(f)(1) of the Act, which states that early intervening services are for children in kindergarten through grade 12, with a particular emphasis on children in kindergarten through grade 3." p. 46627

Early Intervening Services, Staff Professional Development

"Section 300.226(b) follows the specific language in section 613(f)(2) of the Act and requires that in implementing co-ordinated, early intervening services, an **LEA** may provide, among other services, professional development for teachers and other personnel to enable such personnel to deliver scientifically based academic and behavioral interventions." p. 46627

Early Intervention Services

"Early intervention services ... are services for children birth through age two that are designed to meet the developmental needs of infants and toddlers with disabilities under section 632 in Part **C** of the Act." p. 46627

Educational Credentials

"There is nothing in the Act that authorizes the Department to require schools to publicly post the credentials of educational personnel or to provide parents with information about the qualification of their child's teachers and other service providers. Section 615 of the Act describes the guaranteed procedural safeguards afforded to children with disabilities and their parents under the Act but does not address whether parents can request information about the qualifications of teachers and other service providers." p. 46561

Educational Records, Challenging

"Sections 300.618, 300.619, and 300.621 all address the process that parents must use to seek changes in their child's records if they believe the record is inaccurate, misleading, or otherwise in violation of the privacy or other rights of the child. When a parent requests that a change be made in the child's record, under § 300.618, agencies must amend the information within a reasonable time or inform parents of the agency's refusal to amend the information and the parent's right to a hearing to challenge the public agency's determination. If parents want to challenge the accuracy of information in the child's education records, they may do so by requesting a hearing under §300.619 (by contacting the LEA staff member assigned that responsibility). Section 300.621 specifically provides that a hearing held under § 300.619 must be conducted according to the procedures in 34 CFR 99.22. 34 CFR 99.22, in turn, requires a hearing to meet the following minimum requirements: (a) The educational agency or institution shall hold the hearing within a reasonable time after it has received the request for the hearing from the parent or eligible student. (b) The educational agency or institution shall give the parent or eligible student notice of the date, time, and place, reasonably in advance of the hearing. (c) The hearing may be conducted by any individual, including an official of the educational agency or institution, who does not have a direct interest in the outcome of the hearing. (d) The educational agency or institution shall give the parent or eligible student a full and fair opportunity to present evidence relevant to the issues raised under §99.21. The parent or eligible student may, at their own expense, be assisted or represented by one or more individuals of his or her own choice, including an attorney. (e) The educational agency or institution shall make its decision in writing within a reasonable period of time after the hearing. (f) The decision must be based solely on the evidence presented at the hearing, and must include a summary of the evidence and the reasons for the decision.

The parent is not required, under the Act and these regulations, to follow the procedures that are applicable to filing a due process complaint under §§ 300.507 through 300.510. This is because the hearing authorized under §300.619 is for the explicit purpose of giving a parent the opportunity to challenge the information in education records when a parent believes the information is inaccurate, misleading, or otherwise in violation of the privacy or other rights of the child. We do not believe further clarification regarding the specific procedures in §§ 300.618 and 300.619 is necessary. The procedures used for these hearings vary from State to State, and we believe it is best to give States the flexibility to develop their own procedures for such hearings, as long as they meet the requirements in § 300.621." p. 46736

Educational Records, Disciplinary

"It is important to clarify that the Act does not require the transmission of student disciplinary information when the child transfers from one school to another. Rather, section 613(i) of the Act allows each State to decide whether to require its public agencies to include disciplinary statements in student records and transmit such statements with student records when a child transfers from one school to another. The State's policy on transmitting disciplinary information must apply to both students with disabilities and students without disabilities." p. 46629

Educational Records, Right to Inspect and Review

"The right to inspect and review records includes the right to a response from the agency to reasonable requests for explanations and interpretations of the records; the right to request that the agency provide copies of the records containing the information if failure to provide those copies would effectively prevent the parent from exercising the right to inspect and review the records; and the right to have a representative of the parent inspect and review the records ... " p. 46645

Part II

Department of
Education

34 CFR Parts 300 and 301
Assistance to States for the Education of
Children With Disabilities and Preschool
Grants for Children With Disabilities:
Final Rule

CHAPTER 4: "EDUCATIONAL SERVICE AGENCY" TO "GENERAL EDUCATION CURRICULUM"

Educational Service Agency

"The definition of educational service agency is based on the provisions in section 602(5) of the Act. The definition was added by the Amendments to the Individuals with Disabilities Education Act in 1997, Pub. L. 105—17, to replace the definition of "intermediate educational unit" (IEU) in section 602(23) of the Act, as in effect prior to June 4, 1997. Educational service agency does not exclude entities that were considered IEUs under prior law. To avoid any confusion about the use of this term, the definition clarifies that educational service agency includes entities that meet the definition of IEU in section 602(23) of the Act as in effect prior to June 4, 1997." p. 46552

"With respect to ESAs, we believe that the provisions in § 300.12 and § 300.28 clarify that ESAs have full responsibility and rights as LEAs, including the provisions in § 300.226 related to early intervening services." p. 46552

Elementary School

"Section 300.13, consistent with section 602(6) of the Act, defines an *elementary school* as a nonprofit institutional day or residential school, including a public elementary charter school, which provides elementary education, as determined under State law." p. 46591

"For purposes of the Act, the definitions of *charter school*, *elementary school*, and *secondary school* in §§ 300.7, 300.13, and 300.36, respectively, require that a public elementary or secondary charter school be a nonprofit entity." p. 46565

Eligibility

" ... [T]he Department believes that eligibility decisions should be made within a reasonable period of time following the completion of an evaluation." p. 46637

"The eligibility group should work toward consensus, but

under § 300.306, the public agency has the ultimate responsibility to determine whether the child is a child with a disability. Parents and school personnel are encouraged to work together in making the eligibility determination." p. 46661

"Section 300.323(c) is a longstanding requirement that a meeting be held to develop the child's IEP within 30 days of determining that a child needs special education and related services." p. 46637

Emerging Best Practices

 See also: Evidence-based practices.

Evaluations

"Evaluations under section 614 of the Act are for the purpose of determining whether a child has a disability and because of that disability needs special education and related services, and for determining the child's special education and related services needs." p. 46548

"We recognize that there could be times when parents request that their parentally-placed child be evaluated by different LEAs if the child is attending a private school that is not in the LEA in which they reside. For example, because most States generally allocate the responsibility for making FAPE available to the LEA in which the child's parents reside, and that could be a different LEA from the LEA in which the child's private school is located, parents could ask two different LEAs to evaluate their child for different purposes at the same time. Although there is nothing in this part that would prohibit parents from re-questing that their child be evaluated by the LEA respon-sible for FAPE for purposes of having a program of FAPE made available to the child at the same time that the par-ents have requested that the LEA where the private school is located evaluate their child for purposes of considering the child for equitable services, we do not encourage this practice." p. 46593

"[W]e do not believe that the child's best interests would be well-served if the parents requested evaluations of their child by the resident school district and the LEA where the private school is located, even though these evaluations are conducted for different purposes. A prac-tice of subjecting a child to repeated testing by separate LEAs in close proximity of time may not be the most ef-fective or desirable way of ensuring that the evaluation is a meaningful measure of whether a child has a disability or of providing an appropriate assessment of the child's educational needs." p. 46593

"An "evaluation," as used in the Act, refers to an individual assessment to determine eligibility for special education and related services, consistent with the evaluation procedures in §§ 300.301 through 300.311." p. 46639

 See also: Initial Evaluations

Evaluation, Independent Educational (IEE)

"An IEE would be considered as a potential source of additional information that the public agency and parent could consider in determining whether the educational or related services needs of the child warrant a reevaluation, but it would not be considered a reevaluation. There is no restriction on when a parent can request an IEE." p. 46641

"An IEE is defined in §300.502(a)(3)(i) as an evaluation conducted by a qualified examiner who is not employed by the public agency responsible for the education of the child in question." p. 46689

"Generally, the purpose of an evaluation under the Act is to determine whether the child is a child with a disability, and in the case of a reevaluation, whether the child continues to have a disability, and the educational needs of the child. It would be inconsistent with the Act for a public agency to limit the scope of an IEE in a way that would prevent an independent evaluator from fulfilling these purposes." p. 46690

"Section 300.305(a) provides that, as part of an initial evaluation (if appropriate) and as part of any reevaluation under this part, the IEP Team and other qualified professionals, as appropriate, must review existing evaluation data on the child, including input from the child's parents. Since the review of existing evaluation data and input from the child's parents are part of the public agency's evaluation, they would also be appropriate elements in an IEE." p. 46690

Evaluation, Initial

"Section 300.300(a)(1)(i), consistent with section 614(a)(1)(D)(i)(I) of the Act, is clear that the public agency proposing to conduct an initial evaluation to determine if a child qualifies as a child with a disability under § 300.8 must obtain consent from the parent of the child before conducting the evaluation." p. 46632.

 See also: Consent

"While we agree that a public agency would not be in

violation of the FAPE requirements for failing to pursue an initial evaluation through due process, we do not believe that a change to the regulations is necessary. The FAPE requirements in §§ 300.101 through 300.112, consistent with section 612(a) of the Act, apply only to a *child with a disability*, as defined in § 300.8 and section 602(3) of the Act. A child would not be considered a child with a disability under the Act if the child has not been evaluated in accordance with §§ 300.301 through 300.311 and determined to have one of the disabilities in § 300.8(a), and because of that disability, needs special education and related services. Further, § 300.534(c)(1), consistent with section 615(k)(5)(C) of the Act, provides that a public agency would not be deemed to have knowledge that a child is a child with a disability, for disciplinary purposes, if a parent has not allowed the child to be evaluated or refuses services under the Act." p. 46632

" ... States and LEAs should not be considered to be in violation of their obligation to locate, identify, and evaluate children suspected of being children with disabilities under § 300.111 and section 612(a)(3) of the Act if they decline to pursue an evaluation (or reevaluation) to which a parent has refused or failed to consent." p. 46632

"If transportation to an evaluation outside the school environment is necessary, the public agency would have to provide it, as a part of its obligation to ensure that all eligible children are located, identified, and evaluated."
p. 46633

"In § 300.301(a), we interpret this language as requiring *public agencies,* as that term is defined in § 300.33, to conduct evaluations, because those are the only agencies in the State responsible for providing **FAPE** to eligible children. The same language is used in section 614(a)(1)(B) of the Act to describe the agencies that may initiate a request for an initial evaluation to determine if a child is a child with a disability. We similarly interpret this language to be referring to the entities that are public agencies under § 300.33." p. 46636

"... [I]t has been the Department's longstanding policy that evaluations be conducted within a reasonable period of time following the agency's receipt of parental consent, if the public agency agrees that an initial evaluation is needed to determine whether a child is a child with a disability." p. 46637

"[A] child's social or cultural background is one of many factors that a public agency must consider in interpreting evaluation data to determine if a child is a child with a disability under § 300.8 and the educational needs of the child, consistent with §300.306(c)(1)(i)." p. 46661

Evaluation, Initiation of

"[P]ersons such as employees of the SEA, LEA, or other public agencies responsible for the education of the child may identify children who might need to be referred for an evaluation. However, it is the parent of a child and the public agency that have the responsibility to initiate the evaluation procedures in §§ 300.301 through 300.311 and section 614 of the Act." p. 46636

Evaluations, Purpose

"Evaluations under section 614 of the Act are for the purpose of determining whether a child has a disability and because of that disability needs special education and related services, and for determining the child's special education and related services needs." p. 46548

"Generally, the purpose of an evaluation ... is to determine whether the child is a child with a disability, and in the case of a reevaluation, whether the child continues to have a disability, and the educational needs of the child."

p. 46690

Evaluation, Telephone Assistive Services

"It would be inappropriate under the Act to reauire evaluations for other purposes or to reauire an evaluation for telephone assistive services for all children with speech and hearing disabilities. However, if it was determined that learning to use telephone assisted services, was an important skill for a particular child (e.g., as part of a transition plan), it would be appropriate to conduct an evaluation of that particular child to determine if the child needed specialized instruction in order to use such services." p. 46548

Evidenced-Based Practices

"Section 300.320(a)(4) incorporates the language in section 614(d)(1)(A)(i)(IV) of the Act, which reauires that special education and related services and supplementary aids and services be based on peer-reviewed research to the extent practicable. The Act does not refer to "evidenced-based practices" or "emerging best practices," which are generally terms of art that may or may not be based on peer reviewed research." p. 46665

"While the Act clearly places an emphasis on practices

that are based on scientific research, there is nothing in the Act that requires all programs provided to children with disabilities to be research-based .with demonstrated effectiveness in addressing the particular needs of a child where not practicable. We do not believe the recommended change should be made because, ultimately, it is the child's IEP Team that determines the special education and related services that are needed by the child in order for the child to receive FAPE." p. 46665

Excess Cost Calculation

" ... [T]he calculation of excess costs may not include capital outlay or debt service." p. 46553

"Express Concern"

"We do not believe it is necessary to clarify the phrase "express concern". in § 300.534(b) because we believe that, in the context of this section, it is understood to mean that a parent is concerned that his or her child is in need of special education and related services and expresses that concern in writing to the child's teacher or administrative personnel." p. 46727

Extended School Year Services.

" ... [D]ays on which ESY services are provided cannot be counted as a *school day*. because ESY services are provided only to children with disabilities." p. 46553

"The right of an individual child with a disability to receive ESY services is based on that child's entitlement to FAPE under section 612(a)(1) of the Act. Some children with disabilities may not receive FAPE unless they receive necessary services during times when other children, both disabled and nondisabled, normally would not be served. We believe it is important to retain the provisions in § 300.106 because it is necessary that public agencies understand their obligation to ensure that children with disabilities who require ESY services in order to receive FAPE have the necessary services available to them, and that individualized determinations. about each disabled child's need for ESY services are made through the IEP process." p. 46582

"Typically, ESY services are provided during the summer months. However, there is nothing in § 300.106 that would limit a public agency from providing ESY services to a child with a disability during times other than the summer, such as before and after regular school hours or during school vacations, if the IEP Team determines that the child requires ESY services during those time periods in order to receive FAPE. The regulations give the IEP Team the flexibility to determine when ESY services are appropriate, depending on the circumstances of the individual child."p. 46582

"The inclusion of the word "only" is intended to be limiting. ESY services must be provided "only" if a child's IEP Team determines, on an individual basis, in accordance with §§ 300.320 through 300.324, that the services are necessary for the provision of FAPE to the child." p. 46582

 See also: School Day

"Extinguished Under State Law"

"The phrase "extinguished under State law" is not used in the Act or these regulations. The phrase was used in the definition of parent in current § 300.20(b)(1). The comparable provision in these regulations is in § 300.30(b)(1), which refers to situations in which the biological or adoptive parent does not have legal authority to make educational decisions for the child." We do not believe that either of these phrases affects the timeliness of decision making by courts regarding parental rights." p. 46568

Fetal Alcohol Syndrome)

"Special education and related services are based on the identified needs of the child and not on the disability category in which the child is classified. We, therefore, do not believe that adding a separate category for children with FAS is necessary to ensure that children with FAS receive the special education and related services designed to meet their unique needs resulting from FAS. We, therefore, do not believe that adding a separate disability category for children with FAS is necessary to ensure that children with FAS receive the special education and related services designed to meet their unique needs resulting from FAS." p. 46549

Free Appropriate Public Education (FAPE)

"The definition of FAPE in § 300.17 accurately reflects the specific language in section 602(9) of the Act ... providing services in conformity with a child's IEP in the LRE is implicit in the definition of FAPE. Consistent with §300.17(b), FAPE means that special education and related services must meet the standards of the SEA and the requirements in Part B of the Act, which include the LRE requirements in §§ 300.114 through 300.118. Additionally, §300.17(d) provides that FAPE means that special education and related services are provided in conformity with an IEP that meets the requirements in section 614(d) of the Act. Consistent with section 614(d)(1)(i)(V) of the Act, the IEP must include a statement of the extent, if any, to which the child will not participate with nondisabled children in the regular education class." p. 46553

"We believe it is unnecessary to change the definition of FAPE ... because providing services in conformity with a child's IEP in the LRE is implicit in the definition of FAPE. Consistent with § 300.17(b), FAPE means that special education and related services must meet the standards of the SEA and the requirements in Part B of the Act, which include the LRE requirements in §§ 300.114 through 300.118. Additionally, § 300.17(d) provides that FAPE means that special education and related services are provided in conformity with an IEP that meets the requirements in section 614(d) of the Act. Consistent with section 614(d)(1)(i)(V) of the Act, the IEP must include a statement of the extent, if any, to which the child will not participate with nondisabled children in the regular education class." p. 46553

"The term FAPE is defined in § 300.17 and section 602(9)(D) of the Act as including, among other elements, special education and related services, provided at no cost to parents, in conformity with an individualized education program (IEP)." p. 46580

"The public agency must make FAPE available until age 21 or the age limit established by State law, even though the child would not be included as graduating for AYP purposes under the ESEA. In practice, though, there is no conflict between the Act and the ESEA, as the Department interprets the ESEA title I regulations to permit States to propose a method for accurately accounting for students who legitimately take longer than the standard number of years to graduate." p. 46581

"The definition of FAPE in § 300.17 is taken directly from section 602(9) of the Act." p. 46582

"FAPE includes not just the special education and related services that a child with a disability receives, but also includes an appropriate preschool, elementary and secondary school education in the State involved. The required special education and related services must be provided at public expense, at no cost to the parent, in accordance with an IEP, and the education provided to the child must meet the standards that apply to educational services provided by the SEA and LEA (except for the highly qualified teacher requirements in §§ 300.18 and 300.156(c)." p. 46598

Due Process, Free, Low Cost, or Other Relevant Services

"The provisions in § 300.507(b) ... require the public agency to inform parents about the availability of free or low-cost legal and other relevant services, if the parent requests such information or the parent or the agency requests a due process hearing. Generally, "other relevant services" refers to other sources that parents could consult for information, such as parent centers." p. 46697

Fails to Respond

"The meaning of "fails to respond," in this context, is generally understood to mean that, in spite of a public agency's efforts to obtain consent for an initial evaluation, the parent has not indicated whether the parent consents or refuses consent to the evaluation." p. 46632

Functional, Functional Skills, Functional Limitations

"We do not believe it is necessary to include a definition of "functional" in these regulations because the word is generally used to refer to activities and skills that are not considered academic or related to a child's academic achievement as measured on Statewide achievement tests. There is nothing in the Act that would prohibit a State from defining "functional," as long as the definition and its use are consistent with the Act." p. 46579

"It is not necessary to include a definition of "functional" in these regulations because we believe it is a term that is generally understood to refer to skills or activities that are not considered academic or related to a child's academic achievement. Instead, "functional" is often used in the context of routine activities of everyday living. We do not believe it is necessary to include examples of functional skills in the regulations because the range of functional skills is as varied as the individual needs of children with disabilities." p. 46661

General Education Curriculum

"As the term "general education curriculum" is used throughout the Act and in these regulations, the clear implication is that there is an education curriculum that is applicable to all children and that this curriculum is based on the State's academic content standards." p. 46579

CHAPTER 5: "Grade 12" to "Interim Alternative Educational Setting"

Grade 12

"The term "grade 12" in the definition of secondary school has the meaning given it under State law. It is not intended to impose a Federal limit on the number of years a child with a disability is allowed to complete his or her secondary education, as some children with disabilities may need more than 12 school years to complete their education." p. 46577

Grade Level Standards

"The reference to "State-approved grade-level standards" is intended to emphasize the alignment of the Act and the ESEA, as well as to cover children who have been retained in a grade, since age level expectations may not be appropriate for these children." p. 46652

Guardians with Limited Appointments

"[G]uardians with limited appointments that do not qualify them to act as a parent of the child generally, or do not authorize them to make educational decisions for the child, should not be considered to be a parent within the meaning of these regulations. What is important is the legal authority granted to individuals appointed by a court, and not the term used to identify them." p. 46566

Guardian Ad Litem

"Whether a person appointed as a guardian ad litem has the requisite authority to be considered a parent under this section depends on State law and the nature of the person's appointment." p. 46566

Hearing Aid

"The decision of whether a hearing aid is an assistive technology device is a determination that is made on an individual basis by the child's IEP Team. However, even if the IEP Team determines that a hearing aid is an assistive technology device, within the meaning of § 300.5, for a particular child, the public agency is responsible for the provision of the assistive technology device as part of FAPE, only if, as specified in § 300.105, the device is required as part of the child's special education defined in §300.39, related services defined in § 300.34, or supplementary aids and services defined in § 300.42." p. 46581

High School Diploma

"[A] regular high school diploma does not include an alternative degree that is not fully aligned with the State's academic standards, such as a certificate or general educational development (GED) credential." p. 46580

"... [A]s noted in the *Analysis of Comments and Changes* section for subpart B, we have clarified in §300.101(a)(3)(iv) that a regular diploma does not include alternate degrees, such as a general educational development (GED) credential." p. 46656

Highly Qualified Special Education Teacher

☞ On December 10, 2015, Every Student Succeeds Act (ESSA) reauthorized the Elementary and Secondary Education Act of 1965 (ESEA). The ESSA amended the IDEA by removing the definition of "highly qualified" in section 605(10) and the requirement that every special education teacher be "highly qualified" by a specific deadline.

Home Schooled Children

"Whether home-schooled children with disabilities are considered parentally-placed private school children with disabilities is a matter left to State law. Children with disabilities in home schools or home day cares must be treated in the same way as other parentally-placed private school children with disabilities for purposes of Part B of the Act only if the State recognizes home schools or home day cares as private elementary schools or secondary schools." p. 46594

Homeless Children

"The term homeless children is defined in the McKinney-Vento Homeless Assistance Act. For the reasons set forth earlier in this notice, we are not adding the definitions of other statutes to these regulations. However, we will include the current definition of homeless children in section 725 (42 U.S.C. 11434a) of the McKinney-Vento Homeless Assistance Act, as amended, 42 U.S.C. 11431 et seq. (McKinney-Vento Act) here for reference.

The term homeless children and youths—

(A) means individuals who lack a fixed, regular, and adequate nighttime residence (within the meaning of section 103(a)(1)); and

(B) includes— (i) children and youths who are sharing the housing of other persons due to loss of housing, economic hardship, or a similar reason; are living in motels, hotels, trailer parks, or camping grounds due to the lack of alternative adequate accommodations; are living in emergency or transitional shelters; are abandoned in hospitals; or are awaiting foster care placement;

(ii) children and youths who have a primary nighttime residence that is a public or private place not designed for or ordinarily used as a regular sleeping accommodation for human beings (within the meaning of section 103(a)(2)(C));

(iii) children and youths who are living in cars, parks, public spaces, abandoned buildings, substandard housing, bus or train stations, or similar settings; and

(iv) migratory children (as such term is defined in section 1309 of the Elementary and Secondary Education Act of 1965) who qualify as homeless for the purposes of this subtitle because the children are living in circumstances described in clauses (i) through (iii)." pp. 46562–46563

Independent Living

"Beginning not later than the first IEP to be in effect when the child turns 16 years of age, section 614(d)(1)(A)(i)(VIII)(aa) of the Act requires a child's IEP to include measurable postsecondary goals in the areas of training, education, and employment and, where appropriate, independent living skills. Therefore, the only area in which postsecondary goals are not required in the IEP is in the area of independent living skills. Goals in the area of independent living are required only if appropriate. It is up to the child's IEP Team to determine whether IEP goals related to the development of independent living skills are appropriate and necessary for the child to receive FAPE." p. 46668

 See also: Socialization, Transition

Individual Education Plan (IEP)

"[Section] 300.323(c)(2) requires that, as soon as possible

following the development of an IEP, special education and related services are made available to the child in accordance with the child's IEP." p. 46587

"With regard to the total timeframe from referral to IEP development, this will vary based on a number of factors, including the timing of parental consent following referral for an evaluation and whether a State establishes its own timeframe to conduct an initial evaluation." p. 46637.

"There is nothing in the Act that limits States and LEAs from adding elements to the IEP, so long as the elements are not inconsistent with the Act or these regulations, and States do not interpret the Act to require these additional elements. Section 300.320(d), consistent with section 614(d)(1)(A)(ii)(I) of the Act, does not prohibit States or LEAs from requiring IEPs to include information beyond that which is explicitly required in section 614 of the Act. However, if a State requires IEPs to include information beyond that which is explicitly required in section 614 of the Act, the State must identify in writing to its LEAs and the Secretary that it is a State-imposed requirement and not one based on the Act or these regulations, consistent with § 300.199(a)(2) and section 608(a)(2) of the Act." p. 46669

"The requirement to conduct a meeting to develop a child's IEP within 30 days of the determination that a child needs special education and related services is longstanding, and has been included in the regulations since they were first issued in final form in 1977 ... Experience has demonstrated that the 30-day timeline for conducting a meeting to develop an IEP is a reasonable time to provide both public agencies and parents the opportunity to ensure that required participants can be present at the IEP Team meeting." p. 46680

IEP, Accessable to Staff

"Section 300.323(d) requires that the child's IEP be accessible to each regular education teacher, special education teacher, related services provider, and any other service provider who is responsible for its implementation. The purpose of this requirement is to ensure that teachers and providers understand their specific responsibilities for implementing an IEP, including any accommodations or supports that may be needed." p. 46681

IEP Meetings

"A public agency is not required to convene an IEP Team meeting before it proposes a change in the identification, evaluation, or educational placement of the child, or the provision of FAPE to the child. The proposal, however, triggers the obligation to convene an IEP Team meeting. Providing prior written notice in advance of meetings could suggest, in some circumstances, that the public agency's proposal was improperly arrived at before the meeting and without parent input." p. 46691

" ... [I]t should be noted that if a public agency wishes to invite officials from another agency, such as officials of the child welfare agency that are not representing the child, the public agency must obtain parental consent for the individual to participate in the IEP Team meeting because confidential information about the child from the child's education records would be shared at the meeting." p. 46669

"Generally, a child with a disability should attend the IEP Team meeting if the parent decides that it is appropriate for the child to do so." p. 46671

IEP Services, Duration, Length of, and Modifications

"The meaning of the term "duration" will vary, depending on such things as the needs of the child, the service being provided, the particular format used in an IEP, and how the child's day and IEP are structured. What is required is that the IEP include information about the amount of services that will be provided to the child, so that the level of the agency's commitment of resources will be clear to parents and other IEP Team members. The amount of time to be committed to each of the various services to be provided must be appropriate to the specific service, and clearly stated in the IEP in a manner that can be understood by all involved in the development and implementation of the IEP." p. 46667

IEP Team, Qualified Professionals

"Section 300.305(d)(1) follows the specific language in section 614(c)(1) of the Act and refers to the decision made by the IEP Team and "other qualified professionals, as appropriate" regarding whether additional data are needed to determine whether a child continues to be a child with a disability and the child's educational needs. The phrase, "qualified professionals, as appropriate" is used to provide flexibility for public agencies to include other professionals who may not be a part of the child's IEP Team in the group that determines if additional data are needed to make an eligibility determination and determine the child's educational needs." p. 46644

"It would be inappropriate to require that individuals with specific professional knowledge or qualifications attend all IEP Team meetings. These decisions should be made on a case-by-case basis in light of the needs of a particular child. Section 300.321(a)(6), consistent with section 614(d)(1)(B)(vi) of the Act, already allows other individuals who have knowledge or special expertise regarding the child, including related services personnel, as appropriate, to be included as members of a child's IEP Team at the discretion of the parent or the agency." p. 46669

Infant or Toddler with a Disability

"Section 632(5)(A) of the Act defines *infant or toddler with a disability* as a child under the age of three years who (a) is experiencing developmental delays in one or more of the areas of cognitive development, physical development, communication development, social or emotional development, and adaptive development, or (b) has a diagnosed physical or mental condition that has a high probability of resulting in developmental delay. In addition, some States also provide early intervention services to infants and toddlers who are at risk of having a developmental delay." p. 46627

94

Informed Consent

 See: Consent

Initial Provision of Services

" ... [T]he "initial provision of services" means the first time a parent is offered special education and related services after the child has been evaluated in accordance with the procedures in §§ 300.301 through 300.311, and has been determined to be a child with a disability, as defined in § 300.8." p. 46633

Intellectual Development

"The reference to "intellectual development" in this provision means that the child exhibits a pattern of strengths and weaknesses in performance relative to a standard of intellectual development such as commonly measured by IQ tests. Use of the term is consistent with the discretion provided in the Act in allowing the continued use of discrepancy models." p. 46651

Interim Alternative Educational Setting

"Section 615(k)(2) of the Act provides that the IEP Team is responsible for determining the interim alternative educational setting for a child with a disability for certain removals that are a change of placement. In § 300.531, for reasons described elsewhere in this preamble, we interpret this obligation to apply to all removals that constitute a change of placement for disciplinary reasons, as defined in § 300.536." p. 46719

"We interpret "setting" in this context to be the environment in which the child will receive services, such as an alternative school, alternative classroom, or home setting. In many instances, the location and the setting or environment in which the child will receive services are the same. It is possible, however, that a school may have available more than one location that meets the criteria of the setting chosen by the IEP Team. For example, an LEA may have available two alternative schools that meet the criteria of the interim alternative educational setting chosen by the IEP Team. In those cases school personnel would be able to assign the child to either of these locations, if the IEP Team has not specified a particular one." p. 46719

"Section 615(k)(2) of the Act provides that the IEP Team is responsible for determining the interim alternative educational setting for a child with a disability for certain removals that are a change of placement. In § 300.531, for reasons described elsewhere in this preamble, we interpret this obligation to apply to all removals that constitute a change of placement for disciplinary reasons, as defined in § 300.536." p. 46719

"What constitutes an appropriate interim alternative educational setting will depend on the circumstances of each individual case." p. 46722

CHAPTER 6: "Indian and Indian Tribe" to "Notice Requirement Purpose"

Indian and Indian Tribe

"The definitions of Indian and Indian tribe are included in sections 602(12) and (13) of the Act, respectively, and are, therefore, included in subpart A of these regulations. Subpart A includes definitions for those terms and phrases about which we are frequently asked and which we believe will assist SEAs and LEAs in implementing the requirements of the Act. Including the definitions of Indian and Indian tribe in the definitions section does not in any way affect the provision of FAPE to all eligible children under the Act." p. 46563

"Section 602(13) of the Act and § 300.21(b) define Indian tribe as "any Federal or State Indian tribe" and do not exclude State Indian tribes that are not federally-recognized tribes." p. 46563

"As defined in § 300.28(b), *local educational agency* or *LEA* includes ESAs and any other public institution or agency having administrative control and direction of a public elementary school or secondary school, including a public nonprofit charter school that is established as an LEA under State law." p. 46627

Institution of Higher Learning

"The term institution of higher education is defined in section 101 of the Higher Education Act of 1965, as amended, 20 U.S.C. 1021 et seq. (HEA)." p. 46564

"The Act does not include specific institutions in the definition of institution of higher education, nor do we believe it is necessary to add specific institutions to the definition in § 300.26." p. 46564

Instructional Methodologies

"There is nothing in the Act that requires an IEP to include specific instructional methodologies. Therefore, consistent with section 614(d)(1)(A)(ii)(I) of the Act, we cannot interpret section 614 of the Act to require that all elements of a program provided to a child be included in an

IEP. The Department's longstanding position on including instructional methodologies in a child's IEP is that it is an IEP Team's decision. Therefore, if an IEP Team determines that specific instructional methods are necessary for the child to receive FAPE, the instructional methods may be addressed in the IEP." p. 46665

Interpreting Services

"The definition of interpreting services is sufficiently broad to include American sign language and sign language systems ... We believe it is important to include sign language transliteration (e.g., translation systems such as Signed Exact English and Contact Signing), in addition to sign language interpretation of another language (e.g., American sign language) in the definition of interpreting services ..." p. 46572

"*Interpreting services*", as defined in § 300.34(c)(4), clearly states that interpreting services are used with children who are deaf and hard of hearing. Therefore, a child who is not deaf or hard of hearing, but who is without expressive speech, would not be considered eligible to receive interpreting services as defined in §300.34(c)(4)." p. 46572

"The definition of interpreting services clearly states that

interpreting services are used with children who are deaf or hard of hearing. The nature and type of interpreting services required for children who are deaf or hard of hearing and also limited in English proficiency are to be determined by reference to the Department's regulations and policies regarding students with limited English proficiency."
p. 46572

"Although the definition of *interpreting services* is written broadly to include other types of interpreting services, we believe that it is important to include in the definition services in which oral communications are transcribed into real-time text ... We also believe that it is important that the definition of *interpreting services* include services for children who are deaf-blind. However, because there are many types of interpreting services for children who are deaf-blind, in addition to tactile and close vision interpreting services, we will add a more general statement to include interpreting services for children who are deaf-blind, rather than listing all the different methods that might be used for children who are deaf-blind." p. 46572

Jurisdictional Issues

"It is important for public agencies to include an explanation of the State complaint procedures in §§ 300.151

through 300.153 and the due process complaint procedures in § 300.507 in the procedural safeguards notice to assist parents in understanding the differences between these procedures. The reference to "jurisdictional issues" addresses the scope of the State complaint and due process complaint procedures." p. 46694

Limited English Proficiency

"The term limited English proficient is defined in the ESEA ... The term *limited English proficient* when used with respect to an individual, means an individual— (A) Who is aged 3 through 21; (B) Who is enrolled or preparing to enroll in an elementary school or secondary school; (C)(i) who was not born in the United States or whose native language is a language other than English; (ii)(I) who is a Native American or Alaska Native, or a native resident of the outlying areas; and (II) who comes from an environment where a language other than English has had a significant impact on the individual's level of English language proficiency; or (iii) who is migratory, whose native language is a language other than English, and who comes from an environment where a language other than English is dominant; and (D) whose difficulties in speaking, reading, writing, or understanding the English language may be sufficient to deny the individual— (i) the ability to meet the State's proficient level of achievement on State assessments described in section 1111(b)(3); (ii) the ability to successfully achieve in classrooms where the language of instruction is English; or (iii) the opportunity to participate fully in society." pp. 46564–46565

"Section 300.306(b)(1)(iii), consistent with section 614(b)(5)(C) of the Act, clearly states that limited English proficiency cannot be the basis for determining a child to be a child with a disability under any of the disability categories in § 300.8." p. 46551

Local Educational Agency (LEA)

"As defined in § 300.28(b), *local educational agency or LEA* includes ESAs and any other public institution or agency having administrative control and direction of a public elementary school or secondary school, including a public nonprofit charter school that is established as an LEA under State law." p. 46627

Local Educational Agency (LEA), Including the Bureau of Indiana Affairs (BIA) Funded Schools

"The definition of local educational agency in § 300.28 and section 602(19) of the Act, including the provision on BIA

funded schools in section 602(19)(C) of the Act and in §
300.28(c), states that the term "LEA" includes an elementary school or secondary school funded by the BIA,
"but only to the extent that the inclusion makes the
school eligible for programs for which specific eligibility is
not provided to the school in another provision of law and
the school does not have a student population that is
smaller than the student population of the LEA receiving
assistance under the Act with the smallest student population." Therefore, BIA schools do not have full responsibility and rights as LEAs under all provisions of the Act."
p. 46553

"The definition of LEA in § 300.28(b)(2) specifically includes a public charter school that is established as an
LEA under State law and that exercises administrative
control or direction of, or performs a service function for,
itself." p. 46565

Locate

"Locate," as used in §300.519(a)(2), regarding a public
agency's efforts to locate a child's parent, means that a
public agency makes reasonable efforts to discover the
whereabouts of a parent, as defined in § 300.30, before as-
signing a surrogate parent. We do not believe that it is

necessary to define "locate" in these regulations because it has the same meaning as the common meaning of the term." p. 46710

Manifestation Determination Meeting

"Under section 615(k)(1)(F) of the Act and section 504 of the Rehabilitation Act of 1973, if the behavior that resulted in the is determined to be a manifestation of a child's disability, the child must be returned to the placement from which the child was removed (other than a 45-day placement under §§ 300.530(g), 300.532(b)(2), and 300.533), unless the public agency and the parents otherwise agree to a change of placement." p. 46720

"As provided in § 300.530(e), a manifestation determination is only required for disciplinary removals that constitute a change of placement under § 300.536. However, we must recognize that Congress specifically removed from the Act a requirement to conduct a functional behavioral assessment or review and modify an existing behavioral intervention plan for all children within 10 days of a disciplinary removal, regardless of whether the behavior was a manifestation or not." p. 46721

Mediation

"Section 615(e)(2)(F) of the Act and § 300.506(b)(7) clarify that an agreement reached through mediation is a legally binding document enforceable in State and Federal courts. Therefore, an agreement reached through mediation is not subject to the SEA's approval." p. 46605

Medicaid, Private Insurance, Other Public Benefits

"Section 300.154(d)(2)(iv) has been changed to clarify that consent must be obtained each time the public agency seeks to access a parent's public benefits or insurance and to clarify that a parent's refusal to allow access to the parent's public benefits or insurance does not relieve the public agency of its responsibility to ensure that all required services are provided at no cost to the parent." p. 46608

"... [I]t is important to let parents know that their refusal to allow access to their public benefits or insurance does not relieve the public agency of its responsibility to ensure that all required services are provided at no cost to the parents." p. 46608

"We do not believe further clarification is necessary

because § 300.154(d)(2) is sufficiently clear that the child's receipt of Medicaid -funded educational services, consistent with the Act and these regulations, should not deny the child receipt of other services for which he or she may be eligible under Medicaid or other noneducational programs. Further, § 300.103(b) provides that nothing in part 300 relieves an insurer or third party from an otherwise valid obligation to pay for services provided to a child with a disability." p. 46609

" ... [Section] 300.154(d)(2) is sufficiently clear that the child's receipt of Medicaid-funded educational services, consistent with the Act and these regulations, should not deny the child receipt of other services for which he or she may be eligible under Medicaid or other noneducational programs. Further, § 300.103(b) provides that nothing in part 300 relieves an insurer or third party from an otherwise valid obligation to pay for services provided to a child with a disability." p. 46609

"Section 300.156, consistent with section 612(a)(14)(B)(i) of the Act, clarifies that it is up to each SEA to establish qualifications for personnel to carry out the purposes of the Act. This will require weighing the various policy concerns unique to each State. The qualifications of related services providers required under Medicaid, or in hospitals

107

and other public settings, and the fact that Medicaid will not pay for providers who do not meet Medicaid provider qualifications should serve as an incentive for States that want to bill for medical services on children's IEPs to impose consistent requirements for qualifications of related services providers." p. 46610

"LEAs are not obligated under the Act to participate in a State Medicaid program. Title XIX of the Social Security Act of 1965, as amended, controls Medicaid reimbursement for medical assistance for eligible individuals and families with low incomes and resources." p. 46740

Medical Services

"Section 602(26) of the Act also stipulates that only medical services that are for diagnostic and evaluative purposes and required to assist a child with a disability to benefit from special education are considered a *related service*." p. 46581

Mental Retardation

" ... [T]the definition of mental retardation ... is defined broadly enough in § 300.8(c)(6) to include a child's functional limitations in specific life areas ... There is nothing in the Act or these regulations that would prevent a State from including ''functional limitations in specific life areas'' in a State's definition of mental retardation, as long as the State's definition is consistent with these regulations.'' p. 46650

Multiple Disabilities

"The definition of multiple disabilities has been in the regulations since 1977 and does not expand eligibility beyond what is provided for in the Act. The definition helps ensure that children with more than one disability are not counted more than once for the annual report of children served because States do not have to decide among two or more disability categories in which to count a child with multiple disabilities." p. 46550

Multiple Subjects

''Multiple subjects'' refers to two or more core academic subjects." p. 46559

"Must" and "Will"

"The word "must" is used ... to clarify that an IEP is required to include the items listed ..." p. 46661

"Generally, we have used the word "must" for regulations that describe what a public agency must do and the word "will" when referring to what the IEP Team has determined a child will do." p. 46666

NIMAC Format, "Publish"

"The duties of the NIMAC are specified in section 674(e)(2) of the Act and include: (a) receiving and maintaining a catalog of print instructional materials prepared in the NIMAS format; (b) providing access to print instructional materials in accessible media, free of charge to blind or other persons with print disabilities in elementary schools and secondary schools; and (c) developing, adopting, and publishing procedures to protect against copyright infringement, with respect to print instructional materials provided under sections 612(a)(23) and 613(a)(6) of the Act.

Section 674(c) of the Act provides that NIMAC's duties apply to print instructional materials published after July 19, 2006, the date on which the final rule establishing the NIMAS is published in the Federal Register (71 FR 41084). The Department interprets "publish" to have the plain meaning of the word, which is to issue for sale or distribution to the public. The NIMAC's duties, therefore, apply to print instructional materials made available to the public for sale after the **NIMAS** is published in the **Federal Register**." However, this does not relieve **SEAs** and **LEAs** of their responsibility to provide accessible instructional materials in a timely manner, regardless of when the instructional materials were 'published'." p. 46620

Native Language

"The definition of native language was expanded in the 1999 regulations to ensure that the full range of needs of children with disabilities whose native language is other than English is appropriately addressed. The definition clarifies that in all direct contact with the child (including an evaluation of the child), native language means the language normally used by the child and not that of the parents, if there is a difference between the two. The definition also clarifies that for individuals with deafness or blindness, or for individuals with no written language, the native language is the mode of communication that is normally used by the individual (such as sign language, Braille, or oral communication)." p. 46565

"Section 300.304(c)(1)(ii), consistent with section 614(b)(3)(A)(ii) of the Act, requires that assessments and other evaluation materials used to assess a child be provided and administered in the child's native language or other mode of communication and in the form most likely to yield accurate information on what the child knows and can do, unless it is clearly not feasible to so provide or administer. We agree that this provision should not be improperly used to limit evaluations in a child's native language, but we do not believe that a change to the regulations is necessary or that it would prevent inappropriate application of the existing rule." p. 46642

Notice Requirement, Purpose

"The purpose of the notice requirement in § 300.322 is to inform parents about the IEP Team meeting and provide them with relevant information (e.g., the purpose, time, and place of the meeting, and who will be in attendance). This is not the same as the procedural safeguards notice that informs parents of their rights under the Act." p. 46678

CHAPTER 7: "Orientation and Mobility Services" to "Per Capita"

Orientation and Mobility Services

"We believe that including travel training in the definition of *orientation and mobility services* may be misinterpreted to mean that travel training is available only for children who are blind or visually impaired or that travel training is the same as orientation and mobility services. We will, therefore, remove travel training from §300.34(c)(7). This change, however, does not diminish the services that are available to children who are blind or visually impaired."

p. 46573

" ... [T}ravel training is not the same as orientation and mobility services and cannot take the place of appropriate orientation and mobility services." p. 46573

 See also: Travel Training and Socialization

Other Health Impairment

"The list of acute or chronic health conditions in the definition of other health impairment is not exhaustive, but rather provides examples of problems that children have that could make them eligible for special education and related services under the category of other health impairment. We decline to include dysphagia, FAS, bipolar disorders, and other organic neurological disorders in the definition of other health impairment because these conditions are commonly understood to be health impairments. However, we do believe that Tourette syndrome is commonly misunderstood to be a behavioral or emotional condition, rather than a neurological condition. Therefore, including Tourette syndrome in the definition of other health impairment may help correct the misperception of Tourette syndrome as a behavioral or conduct disorder and prevent the misdiagnosis of their needs." p. 46550

"We believe the definition of *other health impairment* is

generally understood and that the group of qualified professionals and the parent responsible for determining whether the child is a child with a disability are able to use the criteria in the definition and appropriately identify children who need special education and related services." p. 46551

"... [T]here is nothing in the Act that would prevent a State from requiring a medical evaluation for eligibility under other health impairment, provided the medical evaluation is conducted at no cost to the parent." p. 46551

"We believe that the definition is sufficiently broad to include services for other health impairments, such as dysphagia ... " p. 46576

Other Relevant Services

"The provisions in § 300.507(b) are protected by section 607(b) of the Act and require the public agency to inform parents about the availability of free or low-cost legal and other relevant services, if the parent requests such information or the parent or the agency requests a due process hearing. Generally, "other relevant services" refers to other sources that parents could consult for information, such as parent centers.

The Department believes that parents should have easy access to information about any free or low-cost legal and other relevant services in the area." p. 46697

Paraprofessionals

"Section § 300.156(b) specifically requires the qualifications for paraprofessionals to be consistent with any State-approved or State recognized certification, licensing, registration, or other comparable requirements that apply to the professional discipline in which those personnel are providing special education or related services.

In addition, the ESEA requires that paraprofessionals, including special education paraprofessionals who assist in instruction in title I-funded programs, have at least an associate's degree, have completed at least two years of college, or meet a rigorous standard of quality and demonstrate, through a formal State or local assessment, knowledge of, and the ability to assist in instruction in reading, writing, and mathematics, reading readiness, writing readiness, or mathematics readiness, as appropriate. Paraprofessionals in title I schools do not need to meet these requirements if their role does not involve instructional support, such as special education paraprofessionals who solely provide personal care services. For more

information on the ESEA requirements for paraprofessionals, see 34 CFR 200.58 and section 1119 of the ESEA,
and the Department's nonregulatory guidance, *Title I
Paraprofessionals* (March 1, 2004), which can be found on
the Department's Web site at: http://www.ed.gov/pol-
icy/elsec/guid/paraguidance.pdf.

We believe these requirements are sufficient to ensure
that children with disabilities receive services from
paraprofessionals who are appropriately and adequately
trained. Therefore, we decline to include additional standards for paraprofessionals." p. 46554.

"Section 300.156(b)(2)(iii), consistent with section
612(a)(14)(B)(iii) of the Act, does specifically allow
paraprofessionals and assistants who are appropriately
trained and supervised, in accordance with State law, regulation, or written policy, to assist in providing special education and related services to children with disabilities
under the Act. However, this provision should not be construed to permit or encourage the use of paraprofessionals
as a replacement for teachers or related services providers
who meet State qualification standards. To the contrary,
using paraprofessionals and assistants as teachers or related services providers would be inconsistent with the
State's duty to ensure that personnel necessary to carry

out the purposes of Part B of the Act are appropriately and adequately prepared and trained. Paraprofessionals in public schools are not directly responsible for the provision of special education and related services to children with disabilities; rather, these aides provide special education and related services to children with disabilities only under the supervision of special education and related services personnel." p. 46612

" ... [U]nder § 300.156, consistent with section 612(a)(14) of the Act, SEAs have the responsibility for establishing and maintaining qualifications to ensure that personnel necessary to carry out the purposes of this part are appropriately and adequately prepared and trained. Furthermore, SEAs and LEAs have the flexibility to determine the tasks and activities to be performed by paraprofessionals and assistants, as long as they are consistent with the rights of children with disabilities to FAPE." p. 46612

Parent

"The definition of parent in § 300.30 has been revised to substitute "biological" for "natural" each time it appears in the definition, and to add language clarifying that to be considered a parent under this definition a "guardian" must be a person generally authorized to act as the child's parent, or authorized to make educational decisions for the child." p. 46540

"We understand that many people find the term "natural parent" offensive. We will, therefore, use the term "biological parent" to refer to a non-adoptive parent." p. 46565

"Congress changed the definition of parent in the Act. The definition of parent in these regulations reflects the revised statutory definition of parent in section 602(23) of the Act." p. 46565

"We have replaced the term "natural parent" with "biological parent" in the definition of parent and throughout these regulations." p. 46565

"The biological or adoptive parent would be presumed to be the parent under these regulations, unless a question was raised about their legal authority." p. 46566

"Section 300.30(b)(1) states that when more than one party is qualified under § 300.30(a) to act as the parent, the biological or adoptive parent is presumed to be the parent (unless a judicial decree or order identifies a specific person or persons to act as the parent of a child). The biological or adoptive parent has all the rights and responsibilities of a parent under the Act, and the LEA must provide notice to the parent, accommodate his or her schedule when arranging meetings, and involve the biological or adoptive parent in the education of the child with a disability. Thus, if a child is in foster care (and the foster parent is not prohibited by the State from acting as a parent) and the biological or adoptive parent is attempting to act as a parent, the biological or adoptive parent is presumed to be the parent unless the biological or adoptive parent does not have legal authority to make educational decisions for the child or a judicial decree or order identifies a specific person or persons to act as the parent of a child." p. 46568

"Section 300.30(b)(2) clearly states that if a person is specified in a judicial order or decree to act as the parent for purposes of §300.30, that person would be considered the parent under Part B of the Act." p. 46566

"The statutory language concerning the definition of parent was changed to permit foster parents to be considered a child's parent, unless State law prohibits a foster parent from serving as a parent. The language in the regulations also recognizes that similar restrictions may exist in State regulations or in contractual agreements between a State or local entity and a foster parent, and should be accorded similar deference. We believe it is essential for LEAs to have knowledge of State laws, regulations, and any contractual agreements between a State or local entity and a foster parent to ensure that the requirements in § 300.30(a)(2) are properly implemented. States and LEAs should develop procedures to make this information more readily and easily available so that LEAs do not have to engage in extensive fact finding each time a child with a foster parent enrolls in a school." p. 46566

"The phrase "attempting to act as a parent" is generally meant to refer to situations in which an individual attempts to assume the responsibilities of a parent under the Act. An individual may "attempt to act as a parent" under the Act in many situations; for example, if an individual provides consent for an evaluation or reevaluation, or attends an IEP Team meeting as the child's parent. We do not believe it is necessary or possible to include in these regulations the numerous situations in which an individual may "attempt to act as a parent." p. 46567

"Section 300.30(b) was added to assist schools and public agencies in determining the appropriate person to serve as the parent under Part B of the Act in those difficult situations in which more than one individual is "attempting to act as a parent" and make educational decisions for a child. It recognizes the priority of the biological or adoptive parent and the authority of the courts to make decisions, and does not leave these decisions to school administrators." p. 46567

"Section 300.30(b)(2) specifically states that if a judicial decree or order identifies a person or persons to act as the parent of a child or to make educational decisions on behalf of a child, then that person would be determined to be the parent. It was intended to add clarity about who would be designated a parent when there are competing individuals under § 300.30(a)(1) through (4) who could be considered a parent for purposes of this part. It is not necessary to specify or limit this language to provide that the judicial decree or order applies to specific situations, such as in a custody decree. However, it should not authorize courts to appoint individuals other than those identified in § 300.30(a)(1) through (4) to act as parents under this part. Specific authority for court appointment of individuals to provide consent for initial evaluations in limited circumstances is in § 300.300(a)(2)(c). Authority for court appointment of a surrogate parent in certain situations is in §300.519(c)." p. 46567.

"A private agency that contracts with a public agency for the education or care of the child, in essence, works for the public agency, and therefore, could not act as a parent under the Act." p. 46568

"Section 300.30(b)(1) provides that, when more than one party is qualified to act as a parent, the biological or adoptive parent, when attempting to act as the parent under the Act, must be presumed to be the parent, unless the biological or adoptive parent does not have legal authority to make educational decisions for the child. If a surrogate parent already has been appointed because the public agency, after reasonable efforts, could not locate a parent, the public agency would not have to again attempt to contact other individuals meeting the definition of parent in § 300.30 to seek consent." p. 46631

Parental Consent

 See: Consent

Parents, Court Appointed

"It is not necessary to specify or limit this language to provide that the judicial decree or order applies to specific situations, such as divorce or custody cases. However, it should not authorize courts to appoint individuals other than those identified in §300.30(a)(1) through (4) to act as parents under this part. Specific authority for court appointment of individuals to provide consent for initial evaluations in limited circumstances is in §300.300(a)(2)(c). Authority for court appointment of a surrogate parent in certain situations is in § 300.519(c)." p. 46567

"Section 300.30(b)(2) specifically states that if a judicial decree or order identifies a person or persons to act as the parent of a child or to make educational decisions on behalf of a child, then that person would be determined to be the parent. It was intended to add clarity about who would be designated a parent when there are competing individuals under §300.30(a)(1) through (4) who could be considered a parent for purposes of this part." pp. 46547, 46567

Parent, Divorced

"In situations where the parents of a child are divorced, the parental rights established by the Act apply to both parents, unless a court order or State law specifies otherwise." p. 46568

Parent, Foster

"The statutory language concerning the definition of parent was changed to permit foster parents to be considered a child's parent, unless State law prohibits a foster parent from serving as a parent. The language in the regulations also recognizes that similar restrictions may exist in State regulations or in contractual agreements between a State or local entity and a foster parent, and should be accorded similar deference. We believe it is essential for LEAs to have knowledge of State laws, regulations, and any contractual agreements between a State or local entity and a foster parent to ensure that the requirements in § 300.30(a)(2) are properly implemented. States and LEAs should develop procedures to make this information more readily and easily available so that LEAs do not have to engage in extensive fact finding each time a child with a foster parent enrolls in a school." p. 46566

"Under § 300.30(a)(2), a foster parent can be considered a parent, unless State law, regulations, or contractual obligations with a State or local entity prohibit a foster parent from acting as a parent. However, in cases where a foster parent and a biological or adoptive parent attempt to act as the parent, § 300.30(b)(1) clarifies that the biological or adoptive parent is presumed to be the parent, unless the biological or adoptive parent does not have legal authority to make educational decisions for the child. Section 300.30(b)(2) further clarifies that if a person or persons such as a foster parent or foster parents is specified in a judicial order or decree to act as the parent for purposes of § 300.30, that person would be the parent under Part B of the Act." p. 46567.

" ... [I]f a child is in foster care (and the foster parent is not prohibited by the State from acting as a parent) and the biological or adoptive parent is attempting to act as a parent, the biological or adoptive parent is presumed to be the parent unless the biological or adoptive parent does not have legal authority to make educational decisions for the child or a judicial decree or order identifies a specific person or persons to act as the parent of a child."
p. 46568

" ... [I]f a child has a foster parent who can act as a *parent,* as defined in § 300.30(a)(2), or a person such as a grandparent or step-parent who is legally responsible for the child's welfare, and that person's whereabouts are known or the person can be located after reasonable efforts by the public agency, parental consent would be required for the initial evaluation." p. 46630

"A child with a foster parent who is considered a parent, as defined in § 300.30(a), does not need a surrogate parent unless State law, regulations, or contractual obligations with a State or local entity prohibit a foster parent from acting as a parent, consistent with § 300.30(a)(2)." p. 46712

"Section 300.320(a)(4) incorporates the language in section 614(d)(1)(A)(i)(IV) of the Act, which requires that special education and related services and supplementary aids and services be based on peer-reviewed research to the extent practicable. The Act does not refer to "evidenced-based practices" or "emerging best practices," which are generally terms of art that may or may not be based on peer reviewed research." p. 46665

Pattern of Removals

"We believe it is important for purposes of school safety and order to preserve the authority that school personnel have to be able to remove a child for a discipline infraction for a short period of time, even though the child already may have been removed for more than 10 school days in that school year, as long as the pattern of removals does not itself constitute a change in placement of the child." p. 46715

"Portions of a school day that a child had been suspended may be considered as a removal in regard to determining whether there is a pattern of removals as defined in §300.536." p. 46715

"Whether a pattern of removals constitutes a "change in placement" under ... (proposed § 300.536(b)) must be determined on a case-by-case basis by the public agency. We agree it is important to clarify this position in these regulations and is necessary to ensure proper implementation of this section. We are including the language from the Federal Register of March 12, 1999 (64 FR 12618) ..." pp. 46729-46730

Patterns of Strengths and Weaknesses

"Patterns of strengths and weaknesses commonly refer to the examination of profiles across different tests used historically in the identification of children with SLD. We believe that the meaning of "pattern of strengths and weaknesses" is clear and does not need to be clarified in these regulations." p. 46655

Peer-Reviewed Research

"Peer-reviewed research" generally refers to research that

is reviewed by qualified and independent reviewers to ensure that the quality of the information meets the standards of the field before the research is published. However, there is no single definition of "peer reviewed research" because the review process varies depending on the type of information to be reviewed. We believe it is beyond the scope of these regulations to include a specific definition of "peer-reviewed research" and the various processes used for peer reviews." p. 46664

Per Capita

"We do not believe it is necessary to include a definition of "per capita" in § 300.203(b) because we believe that, in the context of the regulations, it is clear that we are using this term to refer to the amount per child with a disability served by the LEA." p. 46624

CHAPTER 8 — "Personal Items and Devices" to "Reasonable Measures/Efforts"

Personal Items and Devices

"As a general matter, public agencies are not responsible for providing personal devices, such as eyeglasses or hearing aids that a child with a disability requires, regardless of whether the child is attending school. However, if it is not a surgically implanted device and a child's IEP Team determines that the child requires a personal device (e.g., eyeglasses) in order to receive FAPE, the public agency must ensure that the device is provided at no cost to the child's parents." p. 46581

Personnel Qualifications

"Section 300.156, consistent with section 612(a)(14) of the Act, clarifies that it is the responsibility of each State to establish personnel qualifications to ensure that personnel necessary to carry out the purposes of the Act are appropriately and adequately prepared and trained and have the content knowledge and skills to serve children with disabilities. It is not necessary to add more specific functions of individuals providing interpreting services ... States are appropriately given the flexibility to determine the qualifications and responsibilities of personnel, based on the needs of children with disabilities in the State." p. 46572

"Section 300.156, consistent with section 612(a)(14) of the Act, requires each State to establish personnel qualifications to ensure that personnel necessary to carry out the purposes of the Act are appropriately and adequately prepared and trained and have the content knowledge and skills to serve children with disabilities." p. 46573

"Consistent with § 300.156 and section 612(a)(14) of the Act, it is up to each State to establish personnel qualifications to ensure that personnel necessary to carry out the purposes of the Act are appropriately and adequately prepared and trained and have the content knowledge and

skills to serve children with disabilities. Section 300.156(b), consistent with section 614(a)(14)(B) of the Act, specifically requires that these personnel qualifications must include qualifications for related services personnel."
p. 46576

Physical Education

"Section 300.108 describes two considerations that a public agency must take into account to meet the physical education requirements in this section. First, physical education must be made available equally to children with disabilities and children without disabilities. If physical education is not available to all children (*i.e.*, children with and without disabilities), the public agency is not required to make physical education available for children with disabilities (*e.g.*, a district may provide physical education to all children through grade 10, but not to any children in their junior and senior years). Second, if physical education is specially designed to meet the unique needs of a child with a disability and is set out in that child's IEP, those services must be provided whether or not they are provided to other children in the agency." p. 46583

Physical Therapy

" .. [T[he definition of physical therapy is broadly defined and could include therapeutic services for children with degenerative diseases ... There is nothing in the Act that prohibits the provision of therapeutic services for children with degenerative diseases, if the IEP Team determines they are needed for an individual child and, thereby, includes the services in the child's IEP." p. 46573

"The definition of physical therapy has been in the regulations since 1977 and is commonly accepted by SEAs, LEAs, and other public agencies." p. 46573

Placement, Change

"With regard to the commenter's question about whether moving a child from a self-contained classroom to a resource room would be a change of placement, we believe that it would be, as it would change the child's level of interaction with his or her nondisabled peers ... In the example provided by the commenter, generally, if a child is moved from a self-contained classroom to a resource room, it is likely that the child's current IEP cannot be implemented in the resource room, because the educational program in the resource room is likely to be substantially and materially different than the educational program in the self-contained classroom or the educational program in the resource room would change the level of interaction with nondisabled peers. Therefore, this situation would likely be a change of placement under the Act." p. 46644

 See also: "Interim Alternative Educational Setting, "Pattern of Removals," Setting

Placement, Educational

"Historically, we have referred to "placement" as points along the continuum of placement options available for a child with a disability, and "location" as the physical surrounding, such as the classroom, in which a child with a disability receives special education and related services ..." p. 46589

"... [T]he Department's longstanding position [is] that "placement" refers to the provision of special education services, rather than a specific place, such as a specific classroom or specific school." p. 46630

"The terms "educational placement" and "placement" are used throughout the Act, and we have followed the language of the Act whenever possible. We do not believe it is necessary to define "educational placement." Section

300.116, consistent with section 612(a)(5) of the Act, states that the determination of the educational placement of a child with a disability must be based on a child's IEP. The Department's longstanding position is that placement refers to the provision of special education and related services rather than a specific place, such as a specific classroom or specific school." p. 46687

Placement, Residential

"Section 300.104, consistent with section 612(a)(1) and (a)(10)(B) of the Act, is a longstanding provision that applies to placements that are made by public agencies in public and private institutions for educational purposes and clarifies that parents are not required to bear the costs of a public or private residential placement if such placement is determined necessary to provide FAPE. If a public agency determines in an individual situation that a child with a disability cannot receive FAPE from the programs that the public agency conducts and, therefore, placement in a public or private residential program is necessary to provide special education and related services to the child, the program, including non-medical care and room and board, must be at no cost to the parents of the child." p. 46581

"We do not believe it is necessary to further clarify in the regulations that children with disabilities who are placed in residential facilities by public agencies are entitled to FAPE because § 300.146, consistent with section 612(a)(10)(B) of the Act, provides that SEAs must ensure that children with disabilities receive FAPE when they are placed in or referred to private schools or facilities by public agencies." p. 46607

Placement, Stay Put

"The current educational placement during the pendency of any administrative or judicial proceeding described in § 300.518 and section 615(j) of the Act, refers to the setting in which the IEP is currently being implemented. The child's current placement is generally not considered to be location-specific." p. 46709

Placement, Stay Put, During Appeals

"The basis for [§ 300.518(d)] ... is the longstanding judicial interpretation of the Act's pendency provision that when a hearing officer's decision is in agreement with the parent that a change in placement is appropriate, that decision constitutes an agreement by the State agency and the parent for purposes of determining the child's current placement during subsequent appeals. See, e.g., *Burlington School Committee* v. *Dept. of Educ.,* 471 U.S. 359, 372 (1985); *Susquenita School District* v. *Raelee S.,* 96 F.3d 78, 84 (3rd Cir. 1996); *Clovis Unified Sch. Dist.* v. *Cal. Office of Administrative Hearings,* 903 F.2d 635, 641 (9th Cir. 1990). To clarify that ... § 300.518(d) ... does not apply to a first tier due process hearing decision in a State that has two tiers of administrative review, but only to a State-level hearing officer's decision in a one-tier system or State review official's decision in a two tier system that is in favor of a parent's proposed placement, we are removing the reference to "local agency" ..." p. 46710

Placement, Stay Put, Part B

"The Department has long interpreted the current educational placement language in the stay-put provisions in section 615(j) of the Act and § 300.518(a) as referring only to the child's placement under Part B of the Act and not to the early intervention services received by the child under Part C of the Act. We believe that a child who previously received services under Part C of the Act, but has turned three and is no longer eligible under Part C of the Act, and is applying for initial services under Part B of the Act, does not have a "current educational placement.""

p. 46709

Prevailing Party

" ... [W]e believe that the statutory provisions regarding attorneys' fees are appropriately described in § 300.517. Furthermore, section 615(f)(3)(E) of the Act, reflected in § 300.513, recognizes both that hearing officer determinations that a child did not receive FAPE, in some circumstances, may be based on procedural violations, and that hearing officers may order LEAs to comply with procedural requirements. Either of these circumstances, in appropriate cases, might result in a parent being determined to be a prevailing party for purposes of claiming attorneys' fees." p. 46708

Private

"The term *private* is defined in 34 CFR Part 77 ..."
p. 46584

Private School

"The term "private school" as used in § 300.111 means a private *elementary school* or *secondary school*, including a religious school." p. 46584

Private School, Elementary

"If a private preschool or day care program is considered an elementary school, as defined in § 300.13, the child find and equitable services participation requirements in §§ 300.130 through 300.144, consistent with section 612(a)(10) of the Act, apply to children with disabilities aged three through five enrolled by their parents in such programs."
p. 46591

Private School, Equitable Services

"The equitable services made available under Part B of the Act are a benefit to the parentally-placed private school children and not services provided to the private schools."
p. 46595

Private School Services, Parentally Placed Children

"Services offered to parentally-placed private school children with disabilities may be provided on-site at a child's private school, including a religious school, to the extent consistent with law, or at another location. The Department believes, in the interests of the child, LEAs should provide services on site at the child's private school so as not to unduly disrupt the child's educational experience, unless there is a compelling rationale for these services to be provided off-site. The phrase "to the extent consistent with law" is in section 612(a)(10)(A)(i)(III) of the Act. We interpret this language to mean that the provision of services on the premises of a private school takes place in a manner that would not violate the Establishment Clause of the First Amendment to the U.S. Constitution and would not be inconsistent with applicable State constitutions or law. We, therefore, do not have the statutory authority to require that services be provided onsite." p. 46596

Private School Services, State or LEA Placed Children

"If the State or public agency has placed children with disabilities in private schools for purposes of providing FAPE to those children, the State and the public agency must ensure that these children receive the required special education and related services at public expense, at no cost to the parents, in accordance with each child's IEP. It is the responsibility of the public agency to determine whether a particular private school in which the child with a disability will be placed for purposes of providing FAPE meets the standards that apply to the SEA and LEA and that a child placed by a public agency be afforded all the rights, including FAPE, that the child would otherwise have if served by the public agency directly." pp. 46598-46599

" ... [T]he public agency, not the private agency, is responsible for providing FAPE to a child who is placed by the public agency in a private school. Consistent with § 300.146 and section 612(a)(10)(B) of the Act, a public agency that places a child with a disability in a private school or facility as a means of carrying out the requirements of Part B of the Act, must ensure that the child has all the rights of a child with a disability who is served by a public agency, which includes ensuring that the consent requirements in § 300.300 and sections 614(a)(1)(D) and 614(c) of the Act are followed." p. 46599

Private School Services, Transportation

"If services are offered at a site separate from the child's private school, transportation may be necessary to get the child to and from that other site. Failure to provide transportation could effectively deny the child an opportunity to benefit from the services that the LEA has determined through consultation to offer its parentally-placed private school children with disabilities. In this situation, although transportation is not a *related service,* as defined in

§300.34, transportation is necessary to enable the child to participate and to make the offered services accessible to the child." p. 46596

" ... [F]or some children with disabilities, special modifications in transportation may be necessary to address the child's unique needs. If the group developing the child's services plan determines that a parentally-placed private school child with a disability chosen to receive services requires transportation as a related service in order to receive special education services, this transportation service should be included as a related service in the services plan for the child." p. 46597

Private School, Regulatory Authority

"The Act does not give States and other public agencies regulatory authority over private schools and does not place requirements on private schools. The Act imposes requirements on States and public agencies that refer to or place children with disabilities in private schools for the purposes of providing FAPE to those children because the public agency is unable to provide FAPE in a public school or program. The licensing and regulation of private schools are matters of State law." p. 46598

Procedural Safeguards Notice, Changes to

"Section 300.504(c), consistent with section 615(d) of the Act, lists the required contents of the procedural safeguards notice. If these requirements change because of changes made to the Act, public agencies would be required to change their procedural safeguards notice accordingly. Such changes, along with any additional changes to a State's rules, would be subject to the public participation requirements in § 300.165 and section 612(a)(19) of the Act." p. 46693

Procedural Safeguards Notice, Complaints

"The Department intends for parents to receive a copy of the procedural safeguards notice upon receipt of the first State complaint under §§ 300.151 through 300.153 and upon receipt of the first due process complaint under § 300.507 in a school year because we believe that parents particularly need a clear understanding of their rights when they embark on these processes and might not have available copies of the procedural safeguards notice provided earlier in the year, or the notice they previously received may be outdated." p. 46692

"It is important for public agencies to include an

explanation of the State complaint procedures in §§ 300.151 through 300.153 and the due process complaint procedures in § 300.507 in the procedural safeguards notice to assist parents in understanding the differences between these procedures. The reference to "jurisdictional issues" addresses the scope of the State complaint and due process complaint procedures." p. 46694

 See: Jurisdictional Issues

Procedural Safeguards Notice, Disciplinary Actions

"Section 615(k)(1)(H) of the Act requires public agencies to provide parents with a copy of the procedural safeguards notice not later than the date on which the decision to take disciplinary action is made." p. 46692

Procedural Safeguards Notice, Electronic

"Section 300.504(b), incorporates section 615(d)(1)(B) of the Act, and permits, but does not require, a public agency to post a current copy of the procedural safeguards notice on its Web site, if one exists. The public agency would not meet its obligation in § 300.504(a) by simply directing a parent to the Web site. Rather, a public agency must still

offer parents a printed copy of the procedural safeguards notice. If, however, a parent declines the offered printed copy of the notice and indicates a clear preference to obtain the notice electronically on their own from the agency's Web site, it would be reasonable for the public agency to document that it offered a printed copy of the notice that the parent declined. Posting the procedural safeguards notice on a public agency's Web site is clearly optional and for the convenience of the public and does not replace the distribution requirements in the Act."
p. 46693

Procedural Safeguards Notice, IEP Meetings

"The purpose of the notice requirement in § 300.322 is to inform parents about the IEP Team meeting and provide them with relevant information (e.g., the purpose, time, and place of the meeting, and who will be in attendance). This is not the same as the procedural safeguards notice that informs parents of their rights under the Act." p. 46678

Procedural Safeguards Notice, Parents' Mode of Communication

"For parents whose mode of communication is not a written language, §300.503(c)(2) requires the public agency to ensure that the notice is translated orally or by other means to the parent and that the parent understands the content of the notice." p. 46692

Procedural Safeguards, Prior Written Notice

"Section 300.503 already requires prior written notice to be given to the parents of a child with a disability a reasonable time before the public agency proposes (or refuses) to initiate or change the identification, evaluation, or educational placement of the child, or the provision of FAPE to the child. As required in § 300.503(b)(4), the prior written notice must include a statement that the parents have protections under the procedural safeguards of this part. Consistent with §§ 300.503(c) and 300.504(d), the prior written notice and the procedural safeguards notice, respectively, must be written in language understandable to the general public and provided in the native language or other mode of communication of the parent, unless it is clearly not feasible to do so. If the native language or other mode of communication of the parent is not a written language, the public agency must take steps to ensure that the notice is translated orally or by other means to the parent in his or her native language or other mode of communication and that the parent understands the content of the notice." pp. 46688-46689

"Section 300.503(a) ... requires a public agency to provide parents with written notice that meets the requirements in § 300.503(b) a reasonable time before the public agency proposes or refuses to initiate or change the identification, evaluation, or educational placement of the child, or the provision of FAPE to the child ..." p. 46691

"A public agency meets the requirements in § 300.503 so long as the prior written notice is provided a reasonable time before the public agency implements the proposal (or refusal) described in the notice ... Providing prior written notice in advance of meetings could suggest, in some circumstances, that the public agency's proposal was improperly arrived at before the meeting and without parent input." p. 46691

"It is not necessary to explain in the regulations that prior written notice can be provided at the same time as parental consent is requested, because parental consent cannot be obtained without the requisite prior written notice." p. 46691

"There is nothing in the Act or these regulations that would prohibit a public agency from using the IEP as part of the prior written notice so long as the document(s) the

parent receives meet all the requirements in § 300.503."
p. 46691

"When the child with a disability transfers to a new school district, that school district would have an obligation to ensure that the child's parents are provided notice at least once in that school year and at the other times specified in § 300.504(a)." p. 46692

Psychological Services

"The definition of psychological services is sufficiently broad to enable psychologists to be involved in strategies to facilitate social-emotional learning." p. 46573

"Including the development and delivery of positive behavioral intervention strategies in the definition of psychological services is not intended to imply that school psychologists are automatically qualified to perform these duties or to prohibit other qualified personnel from providing these services, consistent with State requirements." p. 46574

Public Agency

"The definition of public agency refers to all agencies responsible for various activities under the Act. The terms "LEA" or "SEA" are used when referring to a subset of public agencies ... [T]he term *public agency* is used only for those situations in which a particular regulation does not apply only to SEAs and LEAs." p. 46569

Public Agency, Conducting Due Process Hearings

"The term "public agency" in these regulations is intended to address situations where an entity might satisfy the definition of *public agency* in § 300.33, but would not satisfy the definition of *LEA* in § 300.28. As set forth in § 300.33, a *public agency* may be responsible for the education of a child with a disability. In these circumstances, the public agency would hold the due process hearing." p. 46705

Public Meeting Notice

"It is unnecessary to include regulations requiring States to provide notice of public hearings in multiple languages and alternative formats. Public agencies are required by other Federal statutes to take appropriate actions to ensure that the public has access, in alternative formats and languages other than English, to public hearings." p. 46614

Reading Instruction, Essential Components

" ... [T]he definition of the essential components of

reading instruction from section 1208(3) of the **ESEA** is included here for reference.

Essential Components of Reading Instruction— The term "essential components of reading instruction" means explicit and systematic instruction in— **(A)** Phonemic awareness; **(B)** Phonics; **(C)** Vocabulary development; **(D)** Reading fluency, including oral reading skills; and **(E)** Reading comprehension strategies. (Section 1208(3) of the **ESEA**)." p. 46646

Reasonable Measures, Reasonable Efforts

"We recognize that the statute uses both "reasonable measures" and "reasonable efforts" when referring to a public agency's responsibility to obtain parental consent for an evaluation, initial services, and a reevaluation. We believe these two phrases, when used in this context, have the same meaning and, therefore, have used "reasonable efforts" throughout the regulations related to parental consent for consistency." p. 46631

CHAPTER 9 — "Recommended Practices" to "Special Education"

Recommended Practices

"The statute and regulations do not refer to "recommended practices," which is a term of art that, generally, refers to practices that the field has adopted as "best practices," and which may or may not be based on evidence from scientifically based research." p. 46627

Recoupment

"The concepts of "recoupment" and "likelihood of regression or retention" have formed the basis for many standards that States use in making **ESY** eligibility determinations and are derived from well-established judicial precedents. (See, for example, *Johnson v. Bixby Independent*

School District 4, 921 F.2d 1022 (10th Cir. 1990); *Crawford v. Pittman*, 708 F.2d 1028 (5th Cir. 1983); *GARC v. McDaniel*, 716 F.2d 1565 (11th Cir. 1983)). States may use recoupment and retention as their sole criteria but they are not limited to these standards and have considerable flexibility in determining eligibility for ESY services and establishing State standards for making ESY determinations. However, whatever standard a State uses must be consistent with the individually-oriented requirements of the Act and may not limit eligibility for ESY services to children with a particular disability category or be applied in a manner that denies children with disabilities who require ESY services in order to receive FAPE access to necessary ESY services."
pp. 46582–46583

 See also: Extended School Year Services

Reevaluations

"It would be inconsistent with the individualized evaluation and reevaluation procedures in section 614(b) and (c) of the Act for a public agency to automatically determine that reevaluations are unnecessary for a specific group of children. In determining whether a reevaluation is needed, the parent and the public agency must consider the child's educational needs, which may include whether the child is participating in the general education curriculum and being assessed appropriately." p. 46640

"It is not necessary to add language clarifying that waiving three year reevaluations must not be a routine agency policy or practice because the regulations are clear that this is a decision that is made individually for each child by the parent of the child and the public agency. Section 300.303(b)(2), consistent with section 614(a)(2)(B)(ii) of the Act, states that a reevaluation must occur at least once every three years, unless the parent and the public agency agree that a reevaluation is unnecessary. When a parent and a public agency agree that a three-year reevaluation is unnecessary, there is no requirement that the public agency offer the parent a reevaluation each year. We do not believe that it is necessary to have such a requirement because if parents who have waived a three year reevaluation later decide to request an evaluation, they can do so. Also, public agencies have a continuing responsibility to request parental consent for a reevaluation if they determine that the child's educational or related services needs warrant a reevaluation." p. 46641

"The review of existing data is part of the reevaluation process. Section 300.305(a), consistent with section 614(c)(1) of the Act, is clear that, as part of any

reevaluation, the IEP Team and other qualified professionals, as appropriate, must review existing evaluation data,
and on the basis of that review, and input from the child's
parents, identify what additional data, if any, are needed
to determine whether the child continues to have a disability, and the educational needs of the child. Therefore,
the opportunity for a parent and the public agency to
agree that a reevaluation is unnecessary occurs before a
reevaluation begins." p. 46641

"As stated in § 300.303, consistent with section 614(a)(2)
of the Act, a parent can request a reevaluation at any
time, and can agree with the public agency to conduct a
reevaluation more frequently than once a year. Likewise, a
parent and a public agency can agree that a reevaluation
is not necessary. We believe that in reaching an agreement
that a reevaluation is unnecessary, as provided for in §
300.303(b), the parent and public agency will discuss the
advantages and disadvantages of conducting a reevaluation, as well as what effect a reevaluation might have on
the child's educational program." p. 46641

Regression, Likelihood of

 See: Recoupment

Regular Education Environment

"It is not necessary to define "regular education environment" or to repeat that children with disabilities should be included in the regular classroom and in nonacademic activities with their nondisabled peers." p. 46670

"[The] "regular educational environment" encompasses regular classrooms and other settings in schools such as lunchrooms and playgrounds in which children without disabilities participate." p. 46585

Regular Education Environment, Preschool

" ... [T]he "regular class" includes a preschool setting with typically developing peers." p. 46666

Related Services

"The definition of related services in § 300.34(b) specifically excludes a medical device that is surgically implanted, the optimization of device functioning, maintenance of the device, or the replacement of that device." p. 46548

"States are in the best position to determine whether a service that is included in the definition of related services should also be considered special education in that State."

p. 46549

"As stated in § 300.34(a), the purpose of related services is to assist a child with a disability to benefit from special education." p. 46574

Relative Contribution

"The phrase "relative contribution," as used in §300.304(b)(3), generally means that assessment instruments that allow the examiner to determine the extent to which a child's behavior is a result of cognitive, behavioral, physical, or developmental factors may be used in evaluating a child in accordance with § 300.304. Because the meaning of "relative contribution" is context specific, we do not believe it should be defined in these regulations."
p. 46642

"Repeatedly Fails" or "Refuses to Produce"

"We do not believe it is appropriate or reasonable to define "repeatedly fails" or "refuses to produce" because the meaning of these phrases will vary depending on the specific circumstances in each case. For example, situations in which a child is absent on the days the evaluation is scheduled because the child is ill would be treated differently than if a parent repeatedly fails to keep scheduled appointments. Similarly, situations in which a parent fails to keep scheduled appointments when a public agency repeatedly schedules the evaluation to accommodate the parent's schedule would be treated differently than situations in which a public agency makes no attempt to accommodate a parent's schedule." p. 46638

Research-Based Intervention

"The Act requires that LEAs be permitted to use a process that determines if a child responds to research-based interventions. Further, there is an evidence base to support the use of *RTI* models to identify children with SLD on a wide scale, including young children and children from minority backgrounds ... *RTI* is only one component of the process to identify children in need of special education and related services. Determining why a child has not responded to *research-based interventions* requires a comprehensive evaluation." p. 46647

"[Section] 300.307(a)(2) ... requires States to permit the use of a process that examines whether the child responds to scientific, *research-based interventions* as part of the information reviewed to determine whether a child has an SLD. The regulations reflect the Department's position on

the identification of children with **SLD** and our support for models that focus on assessments that are related to instruction and promote intervention for identified children."
p. 46647

Resolution Meeting

"Section 615(f)(1)(B) of the Act requires an **LEA** to convene a resolution meeting with the parent and the relevant member(s) of the **IEP** Team within 15 days of receiving notice of the parent's due process complaint. The purpose of the meeting is for the parent to discuss the due process complaint and the facts that form the basis of the due process complaint so that the **LEA** has an opportunity to resolve the dispute. We do not believe it is necessary to require an **LEA** to notify the parent within five days of receiving a due process complaint about the **LEA**'s intention to convene or waive the resolution process. An **LEA** that wishes to engage in a resolution meeting will need to contact the parent to arrange the meeting soon after the due process complaint is received in order to ensure that the resolution meeting is held within 15 days." p. 46700

"Section 615(f)(1)(B)(i)(IV) of the Act states that the purpose of a resolution meeting is for parents to discuss their due process complaint and the facts that form the basis of

the due process complaint so that the **LEA** has an opportunity to resolve the dispute. We do not believe that it is
necessary or appropriate to regulate on the specific struc-
ture or protocol for resolution meetings as doing so could
interfere with the **LEA** and the parent in their efforts to
resolve the complaint in the resolution meeting." p. 466701

 See also: Attorneys' Fees

Response To Intervention

"Section 614(b)(6)(B) of the Act gives **LEAs** the option of
using a process that determines if a child responds to *research-based interventions.*" p. 46647

"Consensus reports and empirical syntheses indicate a
need for major changes in the approach to identifying children with **SLD**. Models that incorporate *RTI* represent a
shift in special education toward goals of better achievement and improved behavioral outcomes for children with
SLD because the children who are identified under such
models are most likely to require special education and related services." p. 46647

"An **RTI** process does not replace the need for a comprehensive evaluation, and a child's eligibility for special education services cannot be changed solely on the basis of

data from an RTI process. Consistent with § 300.303 and section 614(a)(2) of the Act, a child with a disability must be reevaluated if the public agency determines that the educational or related services needs of the child warrant a reevaluation or if the child's parent or teacher requests a reevaluation." p. 46648

"An *RTI* process does not replace the need for a comprehensive evaluation. A public agency must use a variety of data gathering tools and strategies even if an *RTI* process is used. The results of an *RTI* process may be one component of the information reviewed as part of the evaluation procedures required under §§ 300.304 and 300.305. As required in § 300.304(b), consistent with section 614(b)(2) of the Act, an evaluation must include a variety of assessment tools and strategies and cannot rely on any single procedure as the sole criterion for determining eligibility for special education and related services." p. 46648

"There are many RTI models and the regulations are written to accommodate the many different models that are currently in use. The Department does not mandate or endorse any particular model. Rather, the regulations provide States with the flexibility to adopt criteria that best meet local needs." p. 46653

"Section 300.309(c), as revised, clarifies that if a child has not made adequate progress after an appropriate period of time, a referral for an evaluation must be made." p. 46658

 See also: Research-Based Interventions

Results-Oriented Process

The term "results-oriented process," which appears in the statutory definition of transition services, is generally used to refer to a process that focuses on results. Because we are using the plain meaning of the term (i.e., a process that focuses on results), we do not believe it is necessary to define the term in these regulations." p. 46579

Retention

 See also: Recoupment

School Day

"School day, as defined in §300.11(c)(1), is any day or partial day that children are in attendance at school for instructional purposes. If children attend school for only part of a school day and are released early (e.g., on the last day before summer vacation), that day would be considered to be a school day. Section 300.11(c)(2) already defines

school day as having the same meaning for all children, including children with and without disabilities." p. 46552

"Section 300.11(c)(2) ... defines school day as having the
same meaning for all children, including children with and
without disabilities ... [N]on-instructional time (e.g.,recess,
lunch) is not counted as instructional time for a child with
a disability unless such times are counted as instructional
time for all children. Consistent with this requirement,
days on which ESY services are provided cannot be
counted as a school day because ESY services are provided only to children with disabilities." p. 46552

School Health Services, School Nurse Services

" ... [S]chool health services and school nurse services
means health services that are designed to enable a child
with a disability to receive FAPE ... school nurse services
are provided by a qualified school nurse and ... school
health services are provided by either a qualified school
nurse or other qualified person. We recognize that most
schools do not have a qualified school nurse on a full-time
basis (i.e., a nurse that meets the State standards for a
qualified school nurse), and that many schools rely on
other qualified school personnel to provide school health
services under the direction of a school nurse. Therefore,

we believe it is important to retain the definition of *school health services and school nurse services* in these regulations." p. 46574

"As defined in § 300.34(c)(13), *school health services* and *school nurse services* are designed to enable a child with a disability to receive FAPE as described in the child's IEP. A child who is medically fragile and needs school health services or school nurse services in order to receive FAPE must be provided such services, as indicated in the child's IEP." p. 46574

"Section 300.34(a) and section 602(26)(A) of the Act are clear that the definition of related services includes school health services and school nurse services. The IEP Team, of which the parent is an integral member, is responsible for determining the services that are necessary for the child to receive FAPE." p. 46574

"We believe it is necessary to specify that school health services and school nurse services are related services only to the extent that the services allow a child to benefit from special education and enable a child with a disability to receive FAPE." pp. 46574–46575

Scientifically Based Research

"The use of the term scientifically based in § 300.226(b) is intended to be consistent with the definition of the term scientifically based research in section 9101(37) of the ESEA. Because this definition of scientifically based research is important to the implementation of Part B of the Act, a reference to section 9101(37) of the ESEA has been added in new § 300.35, and the full definition of the term has been included in the discussion of new § 300.35. Under the definition, scientifically based research must be accepted by a peer-reviewed journal or approved by a panel of independent experts through a comparably rigorous, objective, and scientific review. We expect that the professional development activities authorized under §300.226(b)(1) will be derived from scientifically based research. The statute and regulations do not refer to "recommended practices," which is a term of art that, generally, refers to practices that the field has adopted as "best practices," and which may or may not be based on evidence from scientifically based research." p. 46627

"The Department does not intend to dictate how extensive the research must be or who, within an LEA or State, should determine that the research is of high quality."

p. 46648

Screening

"Screening," as used in § 300.302 and section 614(a)(1)(E) of the Act, refers to a process that a teacher or specialist uses to determine appropriate instructional strategies. Screening is typically a relatively simple and quick process that can be used with groups of children. Because such screening is not considered an evaluation under §§ 300.301 through 300.311 to determine eligibility for special education services, parental consent is not required." p. 46639

 See also: Evaluations

Secondary School

"For purposes of the Act, the definitions of *charter school*, *elementary school*, and *secondary school* in §§ 300.7, 300.13, and 300.36, respectively, require that a public elementary or secondary charter school be a nonprofit entity." p. 46565

Serious Bodily Injury

"([D]efined in 18 USC 1365(h)(3) as bodily injury), which involve substantial risk of death; extreme physical pain;

protracted and obvious disfigurement; or protracted loss or impairment of the function of a bodily member, organ, or mental faculty." pp. 46722, *See also*: 46723

Services Plan

"The definition of services plan was included to describe the content, development, and implementation of plans for parentally-placed private school children with disabilities who have been designated to receive equitable services. The definition cross-references the specific requirements for the provision of services to parentally-placed private school children with disabilities in § 300.132 and §§ 300.137 through 300.139, which provide that parentally-placed private school children have no individual right to special education and related services and thus are not entitled to FAPE." p. 46577

Significant Disproportionality

"With respect to the definition of significant disproportionality, each State has the discretion to define the term for the LEAs and for the State in general. Therefore, in identifying significant disproportionality, a State may determine statistically significant levels. The State's review of its constituent LEAs' policies, practices, and procedures for identifying and placing children with disabilities would occur in LEAs with significant disproportionality in identification, placement, or discipline, based on the examination of the data. The purpose of this review is to determine if the policies, practices, and procedures are consistent with the Act." p. 46738

"Establishing a national standard for significant disproportionality is not appropriate because there are multiple factors at the State level to consider in making such determinations. For example, States need to consider the population size, the size of individual LEAs, and composition of State population. States are in the best position to evaluate those factors. The Department has provided guidance to States on methods for assessing disproportionality. This guidance can be found at: http://www.ideadata.org/docs/Disproportionality%20Technical%20Assistance%20Guide.pdf." p. 46738

Social Work Services

"Including counseling in the definition of social work services in schools in § 300.34(c)(14) is intended to indicate the types of personnel who assist in this activity and is not intended either to imply that school social workers are automatically qualified to perform counseling or to prohibit other qualified personnel from providing counseling, consistent with State requirements." pp. 46573-46574

"The definition of *social work services in schools* in the 1977 regulations included "mobilizing school and community resources to enable the child to receive maximum benefit from his or her educational program." As explained in the preamble to the final 1992 regulations, the phrase "to receive maximum benefit" was intended only to provide that the purpose of activities carried out by personnel qualified to provide social work services in schools is to mobilize resources so that a child can learn as effectively as possible in his or her educational program. The language in the preamble to the final 1992 regulations also clarified that this provision did not set a legal standard for that program or entitle the child to a particular educational benefit. The preamble further explained that, during the public comment period for the 1992 regulations, commenters raised concerns that the term "maximum benefit" appeared to be inconsistent with the decision by the United States Supreme Court in *Board of Education* v. *Rowley,* 458 U.S. 176 (1982). Therefore, the phrase was revised to read "to learn as effectively as possible in his or her educational program." This is the same phrase used in the 1999 regulations and in these regulations in § 300.34(c)(14)(iv). Because the language in the 1977 final regulations did not entitle a child to any particular benefit, the change made in 1992 did not lessen protections for a child, and, therefore, is not subject to section 607(b) of the Act." p. 46575

"The definition of social work services in schools includes examples of the types of social work services that may be provided. It is not a prescriptive or exhaustive list. The child's IEP Team is responsible for determining whether a child needs social work services, and what specific social work services are needed in order for the child to receive FAPE. Therefore, while conducting a functional behavioral assessment typically precedes developing positive behavioral intervention strategies, we do not believe it is necessary to include functional behavioral assessments in the definition of social work services in schools because providing positive behavioral intervention strategies is just an example of a social work service that might be provided to a child if the child's IEP Team determines that such services are needed for the child to receive FAPE."
p. 46575

Socialization

" ... [Section] 300.324(a)(1)(iv) requires the IEP Team to consider, for all children with disabilities, the academic, developmental, and functional needs of the child, which could include, as appropriate, the child's need to develop skills in the areas of socialization, independent living, and orientation and mobility." p. 46684

Special Education

"We believe the definition of *special education* is clear and consistent with the definition in section 602(20 of the Act. We do not believe it is necessary to change the definition to distinguish special education from the other forms of education ..." p. 46577

"The definition of *special education* ... includes adapted physical education and travel training." p. 46662.

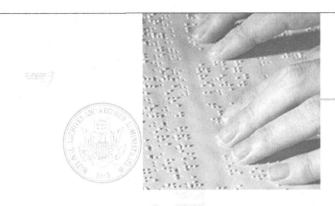

CHAPTER 10: "Specialized Formats" to "Written Informed Consent

Specialized Formats

"*Specialized formats* has the meaning given the term in section 121(d)(4) of title 17, United States Code: (A) Braille, audio, or digital text which is exclusively for use by blind or other persons with disabilities. (B) With respect to print instructional materials, includes large print formats when such materials are distributed exclusively for use by blind or other persons with disabilities." p. 46621

Specially Designed Instruction

"... [Section] 300.39(b)(3) ... defines specially designed instruction as adapting the content, methodology, or delivery of instruction to address the unique needs of the child and to ensure access to the general curriculum so that the child can meet the educational standards within the jurisdiction of the public agency that apply to all children." p. 46577

Specific Learning Disability

"The definition of specific learning disability is consistent with the procedures for evaluating and determining the eligibility of children suspected of having a specific learning disability in §§ 300.307 through 300.311." p. 46551

"Section 602(30) of the Act refers to a "disorder" in one or more of the basic psychological processes and not to a "disability" in one or more of the basic psychological processes." p. 46551

"It is up to each State to develop criteria to determine whether a child has a disability, including whether a particular child has an SLD." p. 46648

"The first element in identifying a child with SLD should be a child's mastery of grade-level content appropriate for the child's age or in relation to State-approved grade-level standards, not abilities. This emphasis is consistent with the focus in the ESEA on the attainment of State-approved grade-level standards for all children. State-approved standards are not expressed as "norms" but represent benchmarks for all children at each grade level. The performance of classmates and peers is not an appropriate standard if most children in a class or school are not meeting State approved standards. Furthermore, using grade-based normative data to make this determination is generally not appropriate for children who have not been permitted to progress to the next academic grade or are otherwise older than their peers. Such a practice may give the illusion of average rates of learning when the child's rate of learning has been below average, resulting in retention. A focus on expectations relative to abilities or classmates simply dilutes expectations for children with disabilities." p. 46652

Although there are additional criteria and procedures for evaluating and identifying children suspected of having SLD, the group must also comply with the procedures and timelines that apply to all evaluations, including evaluations for SLD. Evaluation of children suspected of having SLD must follow the same procedures and timeframes reauired in §§ 300.301 through 300.306, in addition to those in §§ 300.307 through 300.311." p. 46659

State

"The definition of *State* in ... § 300.40 ... is based on section 602(31) of the Act, which does not include an Indian tribe or tribal governing body. Therefore, the Department does not have the authority to interpret ward of the State to include children who are wards of a tribe of competent jurisdiction." p. 46712

State-Approved Standards

"State-approved standards are not expressed as "norms" but represent benchmarks for all children at each grade level. The performance of classmates and peers is not an appropriate standard if most children in a class or school are not meeting State approved standards. Furthermore, using grade-based normative data to make this determination is generally not appropriate for children who have not been permitted to progress to the next academic grade or are otherwise older than their peers. Such a practice may give the illusion of average rates of learning when the child's rate of learning has been below average, resulting in retention. A focus on expectations relative to abilities or classmates simply dilutes expectations for children with disabilities." p. 46652

State Advisory Panel

"The purpose of the State advisory panel, as stated in §300.167 and section 612(a)(21)(A) of the Act, is to provide policy guidance to the SEA with respect to special education and related services for children with disabilities. Pursuant to § 300.168 and section 612(a)(21)(B) of the Act, a broad membership is required. The duties of the panel are, among other things, to advise the SEA on unmet needs, evaluations, and corrective action plans to address findings identified in Federal monitoring reports, consistent with § 300.169 and section 612(a)(21)(D) of the Act. However, although we believe that broad stakeholder involvement in the development of the State performance plans and annual performance reports is very important, we decline to regulate that a specific group be involved in their development. We have, however, provided guidance in OSEP's August 9, 2005 memorandum to States, *Submission of Part B State Performance Plans and Annual Performance Reports,* (OSEP Memo 05– 12), located at

http://www.ed.gov/ policy/speced/guid/idea/bapr/index.html, which directs States to provide information in their State performance plans on how they obtained broad input from stakeholders on the State performance plan." p. 46731

Substantial Bodily Injury

☛ *See:* Serious Bodily Injury

Sufficient Progress Toward Prompt Completion of Evaluations

"The exceptions to the 60- day or State-established timeframe must be permitted because they are statutory. Section 614(a)(1)(C)(ii)(I) of the Act, which is incorporated in § 300.300(d)(2), provides that the 60-day or State-established timeframe does not apply if a child enrolls in a school served by the public agency after the relevant timeframe has begun, and prior to a determination by the child's previous public agency as to whether the child is a child with a disability. The exception applies only if the subsequent public agency is making sufficient progress to ensure prompt completion of the evaluation, and the parent and subsequent public agency agree to a specific time when the evaluation will be completed. We do not believe it is necessary to define the phrase "sufficient progress" because the meaning will vary depending on the specific circumstances in each case ... [T]here may be legitimate reasons for not completing the evaluation within the 60-day timeframe, such as differences in assessment instruments used in the previous and new public agencies, and the length of time between a child leaving one school and enrolling in the next school. Therefore, we believe that whether a new public agency is making sufficient progress to ensure prompt completion of an evaluation is best left to the discretion of State and local officials and parents to determine." p. 46638

Supplemental Instructional Materials

"We agree that supplemental instructional materials may be used, where appropriate, to support early intervening activities. The Conf. Rpt. in note 269 provides that

> [E]arly intervening services should make use of supplemental instructional materials, where appropriate, to support student learning. Children targeted for early intervening services under IDEA are the very students who are most likely to need additional reinforcement to the core curriculum used in the regular classroom. These are in fact the additional instructional materials that have been developed to supplement and therefore strengthen the efficacy of comprehensive core curriculum.

We believe the terms "services" and "supports" in §300.226(b)(2) are broad enough to include the use of supplemental instructional materials." p. 46628

Supplementary Aids and Services

"The definition of supplementary aids and services in ... §300.42 ... is consistent with the specific language in section 602(33) of the Act, and refers to aids, services, and other supports for children with disabilities." p. 46578

"The definition of supplementary aids and services in §300.42 has been modified to specify that aids, services, and other supports are also provided to enable children with disabilities to participate in extracurricular and non-academic settings." p. 46541

" ... [S]upplementary aids and services can be provided in extracurricular and nonacademic settings to enable children with disabilities to be educated with nondisabled children to the maximum extent appropriate." p. 46578

Surrogate Parent

"There is nothing in the Act that would prevent a temporary surrogate parent from having all the rights of a parent. Note 89 of the Conf. Rpt., p. 35810, provides that appropriate staff members of emergency shelters, transitional shelters, independent living programs, and street outreach programs would not be considered to be employees of agencies involved in the education or care of unaccompanied youth (and thus prohibited from serving as a surrogate parent), provided that such a role is temporary until a surrogate parent can be appointed who meets the requirements for a surrogate parent in § 300.519(d). This provision is included in §300.519(f), regarding surrogate parents." p. 46566

"If a child who is a ward of the State already has a person who meets the definition of parent in § 300.30, and that person is willing and able to assume the responsibilities of a parent under the Act, a surrogate parent might not be needed." p. 46566.

"It is not necessary to specify or limit this language to provide that the judicial decree or order applies to specific situations, such as divorce or custody cases. However, it should not authorize courts to appoint individuals other than those identified in §300.30(a)(1) through (4) to act as parents under this part. Specific authority for court appointment of individuals to provide consent for initial evaluations in limited circumstances is in §300.300(a)(2)(c). Authority for court appointment of a surrogate parent in certain situations is in § 300.519(c)." p. 46567

"Students with disabilities in State correctional facilities do not have an automatic right to a surrogate parent solely by reason of their confinement at a correctional facility. Public agencies must make case-by-case determinations in accordance with the requirements in § 300.519, regarding whether a student with a disability in a State correctional facility needs a surrogate parent. Whether a student with a disability confined in a State correctional facility is considered a *ward of the State,* as defined in ... § 300.45 ... whose rights must be protected through the appointment of a surrogate parent, is a matter that must be determined under State law." p. 46710

" ... [P]ublic agencies have a responsibility to ensure that a surrogate parent is carrying out their responsibilities, so there are some circumstances when removal may be appropriate. A mere disagreement with the decisions of a surrogate parent about appropriate services or placements for the child, however, generally would not be sufficient to give rise to a removal, as the role of the surrogate parent is to represent the interests of the child, which may not be the same as the interests of the public agency. We do not think a regulation is necessary, however, as we believe that the rights of the child with a disability are adequately protected under Section 504 of the Rehabilitation Act

(Section 504) and Title II of the Americans with Disabilities Act (Title II), which prohibit retaliation or coercion against any individual who exercises their rights under Federal law for the purpose of assisting children with disabilities by protecting rights protected under those statutes. See, 34 CFR 104.61, referencing 34 CFR 100.7(e); 28 CFR 35.134. These statutes generally prohibit discrimination against individuals on the basis of disability by recipients of Federal financial assistance (Section 504) and prohibit discrimination against individuals on the basis of disability by State and local governments (Title II)." p. 46712

Technical Assistance and Training

"The Department intends the term "training," as used in §300.119, to have its generally accepted meaning. Training is generally agreed to be any activity used to enhance one's skill or knowledge to acquire, maintain, and advance knowledge, skills, and abilities. Given the general understanding of the term "training," we do not believe it is necessary to regulate on this matter." p. 46589

Technical Education

 See: Vocational Education

Technically Sound Instruments

"Technically sound instruments" generally refers to assessments that have been shown through research to be valid and reliable." p. 46642

To The Extent Practicable

"The phrase "to the extent practicable," as used in this context, generally means that services and supports should be based on peer-reviewed research to the extent that it is possible, given the availability of peer-reviewed research." p. 46665

"Special education and related services, and supplementary aids and services based on peer-reviewed research are only required "to the extent practicable." If no such research exists, the service may still be provided, if the IEP Team determines that such services are appropriate. A child with a disability is entitled to the services that are in his or her IEP whether or not they are based on peer-reviewed research. The IEP Team, which includes the child's parent, determines the special education and related services, and supplementary aids and services that are needed by the child to receive FAPE." p. 46665

Transition, Preschool to Elementary School

"We do not believe it is appropriate to clarify in the regulations that the IEP can serve as the services plan because, as stated elsewhere in this preamble, a services plan should only describe the specific special education and related services offered to a parentally-placed private school child with a disability designated to receive services. We believe that using an IEP in lieu of a services plan for these children may not be appropriate in light of the fact that an IEP developed pursuant to section 614(d) of the Act will generally include much more than just those services that a parentally-placed private school child with a disability may receive, if designated to receive services. There is nothing, however, in these regulations that would prevent a State that provides more services to parentally-placed private school children with disabilities than they are required to do under the Act to use an IEP in place of a services plan, consistent with State law." p. 46596

"Although the Act does not specifically require a public agency to provide detailed explanations to the parent of the differences between an IEP and an IFSP, we believe parents need this information to make an informed choice regarding whether to continue to use an IFSP in lieu of an

IEP. Parents, for example, should understand that it is through the IEP that the child is entitled to the special education and related services that the child's IEP Team determines are necessary to enable the child to be involved in and make progress in the general education curriculum and to receive FAPE. If a parent decides to use an IFSP in lieu of an IEP, the parent must understand that the child will not necessarily receive the same services and supports that are afforded under an IEP. For a parent to waive the right to an IEP, informed parental consent is necessary." p. 46680

"For children who are at least three years of age, the IFSP must also include an educational component that promotes school readiness and incorporates preliteracy, language, and numeracy skills. There is no requirement for the IFSP to include all the required elements in an IEP." p. 46680

"Section 300.323(b) outlines the specific requirements that apply when an IFSP is used in lieu of an IEP for children aged three through five, as a means of providing FAPE for the child under Part B of the Act. This is not the same as the policy in section 635(c) of the Act, which gives States the flexibility to provide early intervention services under Part C of the Act to three year old children with disabilities until they enter into, or are eligible under State law to enter into, kindergarten.

Under § 300.323(b), when an IFSP is used in lieu of an IEP, the child continues to receive FAPE. This would not be the case under section 635(c) of the Act. Under section 635(c) of the Act, parents of children with disabilities who are eligible for preschool services under section 619 of the Act and previously received early intervention services under Part C of the Act, may choose to continue early intervention services until the child enters, or is eligible under State law to enter, kindergarten. The option to continue early intervention services is available only in States where the lead agency under Part C of the Act and the SEA have developed and implemented a State policy to provide this option." p. 46680

"Parental consent is required under § 300.323(b), when the IFSP is used in lieu of an IEP, and under section 635(c) of the Act, when a parent opts to continue early intervention services." p. 46680

Transition Services

"We ... do not believe it is necessary for the definition of transition services to refer to all the major life functions or to clarify that functional performance must be a consideration for any child with a disability, and not just for students with significant cognitive disabilities." p. 46579

" ... [T]ransition services must be provided based on a child's age, not the number of years the child has remaining in the child's high school career." p. 46581

"There is nothing in the Act or these regulations that requires a parent or child to participate in transition services that are offered by agencies that the public agency has invited to participate in an IEP Team meeting. However, if the IEP Team determines that such services are necessary to meet the needs of the child, and the services are included on the child's IEP, and the parent (or a child who has reached the age of majority) disagrees with the services, the parent (or the child who has reached the age of majority) can request mediation, file a due process complaint, or file a State complaint to resolve the issue." p. 46671

Travel Training

"Travel training is defined in ... § 300.39(b)(4) ... for children with significant cognitive disabilities and any other children with disabilities who require this instruction, and, therefore, would be available for children who are blind or visually impaired, as determined by the child's IEP Team. Travel training is not the same as orientation and mobility services and is not intended to take the place of appropriate orientation and mobility services." p. 46573

"... [Section] 300.43(a)(4) ... defines travel training to include providing instruction that enables children to learn the skills necessary to move effectively and safely from place to place in school, home, at work and in the community." p. 46577

"We ... do not believe that it is necessary to add travel training to the definition of transition services ... We believe that IEP Teams already consider the importance of transportation and travel training services in the course of planning for a student's postsecondary transition needs. It is unnecessary to state that travel training includes instructing children with disabilities other than blindness, as requested by the commenters, because the definition of travel training already states that travel training is appropriate for any child with a disability who requires this instruction." pp. 46577–46578

Travel Training, Instruction

"Section 300.156, consistent with section 612(a)(14) of the Act, requires each State to establish personnel qualifications to ensure that personnel necessary to carry out the purposes of the Act are appropriately and adequately prepared and trained and have the content knowledge and skills to serve children with disabilities. It is, therefore, the State's responsibility to determine the qualifications that are necessary to provide travel training instruction." p. 46573

"[Section] 300.39(b)(4) ... specifically states that travel training means providing instruction to children with significant cognitive disabilities and any other children with disabilities who require this instruction." p. 46578

Tribal Governing Body

"*Tribal governing body* means, with respect to any school, the tribal governing body, or tribal governing bodies, that represent at least 90 percent of the children served by such school." 25 U.S.C. 2021(19). p. 46741

Unique Circumstances

" ... [W]hat constitutes "unique circumstances" is best determined at the local level by school personnel who know the individual child and all the facts and circumstances regarding a child's behavior. We believe it would impede efforts of school personnel responsible for making a determination as to whether a change in placement for disciplinary purposes is appropriate for a child if the Department attempted to restrict or limit the interpretation of "consider any unique circumstances on a case-by-case-basis." Factors such as a child's disciplinary history, ability to understand consequences, expression of remorse, and supports provided to a child with a disability prior to the violation of a school code could be unique circumstances considered by school personnel when determining whether a disciplinary change in placement is appropriate for a child with a disability. We believe providing school personnel the flexibility to consider whether a change in placement is appropriate for a child with a disability on a case-by-case basis and to determine what unique circumstances should be considered regarding a child who violates a code of conduct, as provided for under section 615(k)(1)(A) of the Act, will limit the inappropriate removal of a child with a disability from his or her current placement to an interim alternative educational setting, another setting, or suspension." p 46714

Universal Design

"The term universal design is defined in the Assistive Technology Act of 1998, as amended. For the reasons set forth earlier in this notice, we are not including in these regulations full definitions of terms that are defined in other statutes. However, we will include the definition of this term from section 3 of the Assistive Technology Act of 1998, as amended, 29 U.S.C. 3002, here for reference." p. 46579

The term universal design means a concept or philosophy for designing and delivering products and services that are usable by people with the widest possible range of functional capabilities, which include products and services that are directly accessible (without requiring assistive technologies) and products and services that are interoperable with assistive technologies." p. 46579

"The definition of universal design is statutory. Congress clearly intended that we use this specific definition when it used this term in the Act." p. 46579

"The definition of *universal design*, as used in the Assistive

Technology Act of 1998, as amended, is included in the *Analysis of Comments and Changes* section for subpart A." p. 46740

Violates a Code of Student Conduct

"Local school personnel have the necessary authority to protect the safety and well-being of all children in their school and, therefore, are in the best position to determine a code of student conduct that is uniform and fair for all children in their school. We, therefore, do not believe it is necessary or appropriate to clarify in § 300.530(a) the meaning of "violates a code of student conduct." p. 46714

Vocational Education

"[Vocational education] is broad in its meaning and generally accepted and understood in the field and, therefore, would encompass such areas as 'career technical' and 'technical education'." p. 46584

Ward of the State

"Section 300.300(a)(2) applies to circumstances in which the child is a ward of the State and is not residing with the child's parents, and requires the public agency to make reasonable efforts to obtain parental consent from the parent for an initial evaluation. The reference to "parent," in this context, refers to anyone who meets the definition of *parent* in § 300.30, consistent with section 614(a)(1)(D)(iii) of the Act." p. 46630

[T]he public agency is not required to obtain informed consent from the parent for an initial evaluation of a child who is a ward of the State and is not living with the child's parent if the rights of the parent to make educational decisions have been subrogated by a judge in accordance with State law and consent for an initial evaluation has been given by an individual appointed by the judge to represent the child. This is a special situation, limited only to children who are wards of the State not living with a parent and limited only to the situation of seeking consent for an initial evaluation. A person appointed under this provision is not a surrogate parent as that term is used in these regulations. The requirements of § 300.519(c) do not apply to persons authorized to provide consent for initial evaluations under this provision." p. 46631

"Whether a student with a disability confined in a State correctional facility is considered a *ward of the State,* as defined in new § 300.45 (proposed § 300.44) whose rights must be protected through the appointment of a surrogate parent, is a matter that must be determined under State law." p. 46710

Written Informed Consent

 See: Consent

August 14, 2006

Part II

Department of
Education

34 CFR Parts 300 and 301
Assistance to States for the Education of
Children With Disabilities and Preschool
Grants for Children With Disabilities:
Final Rule

Monday,
August 14, 2006

Part II

Department of Education

34 CFR Parts 300 and 301
Assistance to States for the Education of
Children With Disabilities and Preschool
Grants for Children With Disabilities;
Final Rule

Monday,
August 14, 2006

Part II

Department of
Education

34 CFR Parts 300 and 301
Assistance to States for the Education of
Children With Disabilities and Preschool
Grants for Children With Disabilities;
Final Rule

ABOUT THE AUTHOR

Pat taught herself to read before she was four. Because of her advanced reding skills, her parents enrolled her in Kindergarten two weeks after turning five years old. They fully expecting her to succeed. That didn't happen.

From the beginning, Pat wondered why she could read better than children several grades above her, but she could not master the most basic math facts. One day she would "get" it, and the next day it was gone.

Six years of tutoring from a licensed teacher did not help. Pat just could not memorize math facts. Arithmetic was a foreign language she could not seem to learn.

Constantly told by her teachers she was lazy, unmotivated, and not working up to her ability, she gave up. Easing through high school with majors in art and business, she believed she was not smart enough to go to college.

Her inability to do the simplest of math haunted Pat into adulthood. She quit several jobs that reauired math. In her twenties, she enrolled in some college credit courses and "aced" them all. She enrolled and was accepted at different times by three colleges. Pat dropped out as soon as her academic advisor said she had to take a math class.

Twenty years later, she enrolled in her fourth college. Immediately, she went to the student services department and asked for testing. To her relief, the tests confirmed her suspicions. Pat was not lazy; she had Dyscalculia, a form of Dyslexia.

Pat was allowed to use a calculator for all classes that require math. With that accommodation, she passed all math and statistics classes with A's and high B's, graduating magna cum laude with a 3.775 GPA.

Pat's difficulties were never about how to apply and analyze math problems. The wiring in her brain somehow failed to give her the ability to do calculations. No one has yet taught her to add, subtract, multiply or divide. To this day, she relies on a calculator.

Pat has an A.S. and a B.A. in Paralegal Studies from Saint Mary-of-the-Woods College, is a member of Lambda Epsilon Chi, an Indiana Registered Paralegal, and an affiliate member of the Indiana and American Bar Associations. She is a nationally known special education Parent Advocate with over 35 years of experience helping families.

A founding Board member of the Council of Parent Attorneys and Advocates (COPAA) and a Commissioner on Tippecanoe County's first Human Rights Commission, Pat also served several terms as president of Tippecanoe Parents and Professionals for Special Education (TPPSE).

In addition to authoring *Special Education: Plain and Simple,* numerous articles she has written are published on the Wrightslaw website. Pat has been a member of its Speakers Bureau since 2005. From 2010 through 2020, she was a faculty member of the College of William and Mary Law School's annual summer Institute of Special Education Advocacy (ISEA) in Williamsburg, Virginia.

Pat is currently a paralegal in the Education Law Division of Connell Michael Kerr Law, LLP, in Carmel, Indiana assisting its Indiana, Texas, Ohio, and Michigan attorneys. She works exclusively in the area of special education, reviewing education and medical records, spotting issues, and drafting due process complaints and other legal documents. She also prepares cases for and assists at hearings and as needed with federal court cases.

Pat lives in the middle of a corn – or bean – field near Odell, Indiana, with her husband, Clark, a retired farmer. She enjoys traveling and playing with her grandchildren and her great-grandchildren.

Made in the USA
Columbia, SC
17 February 2022

55909182R00127